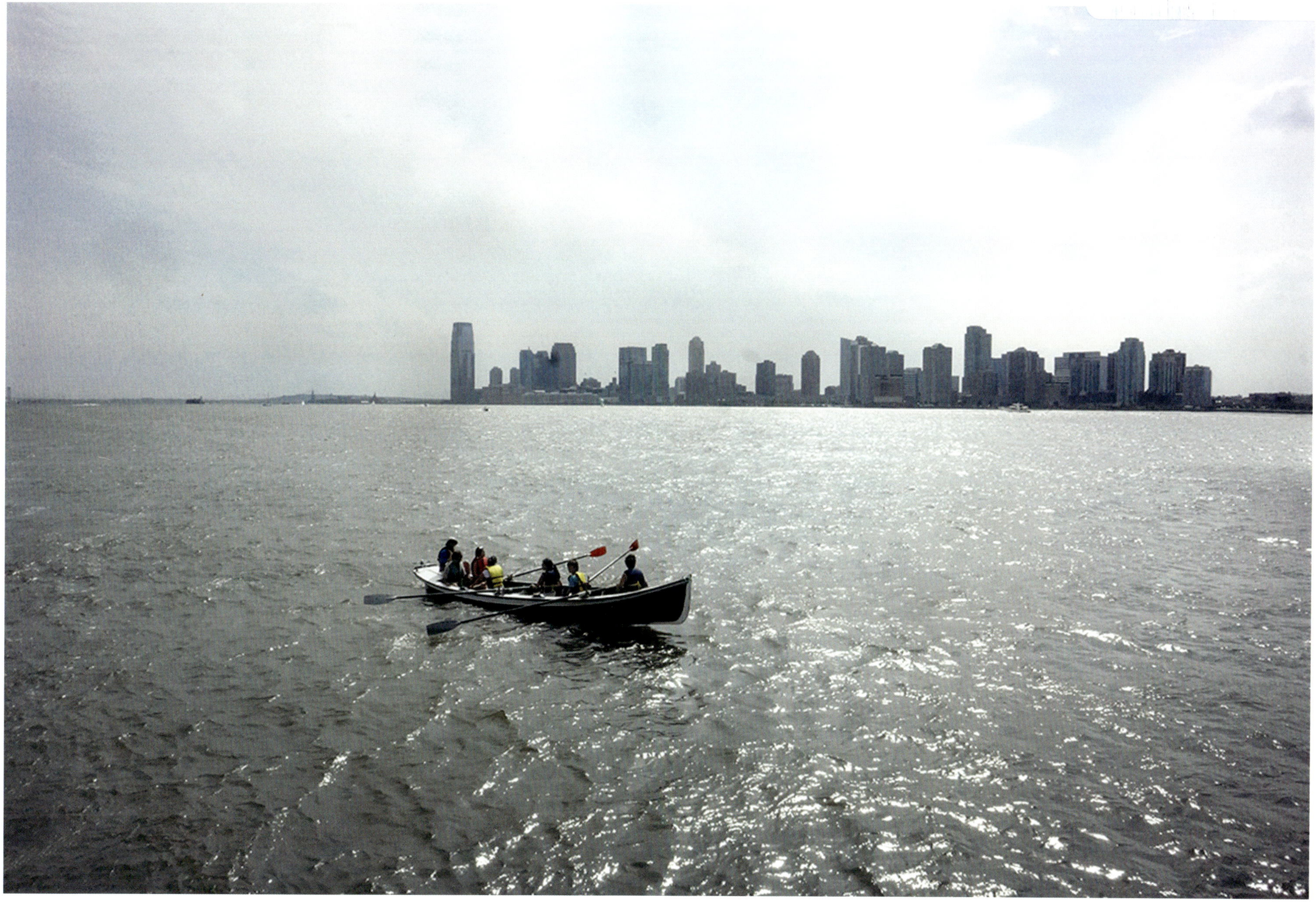

CLOUD CHAMBER

NEW YORK

DAN ZISKIE

DAMIANI

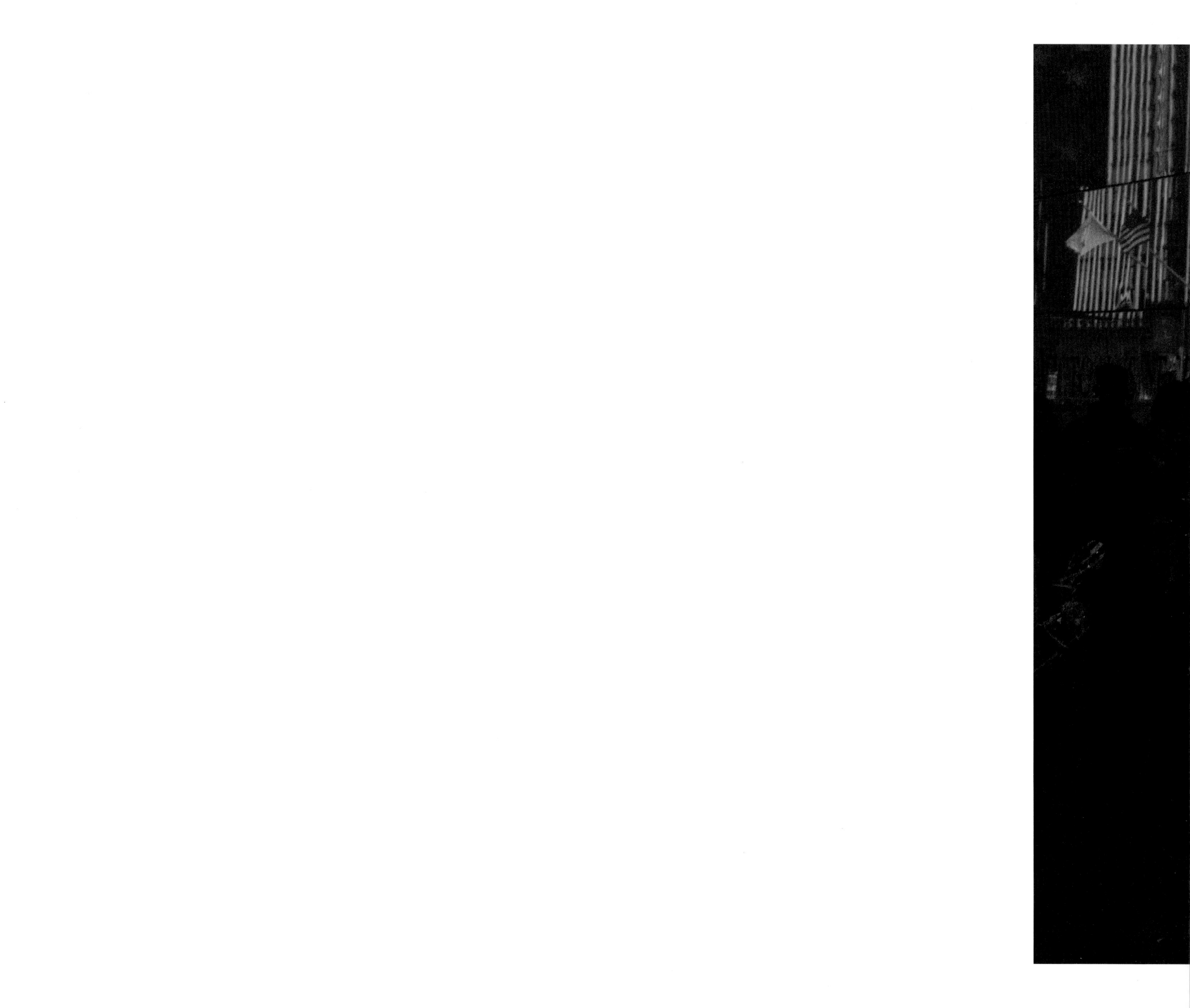

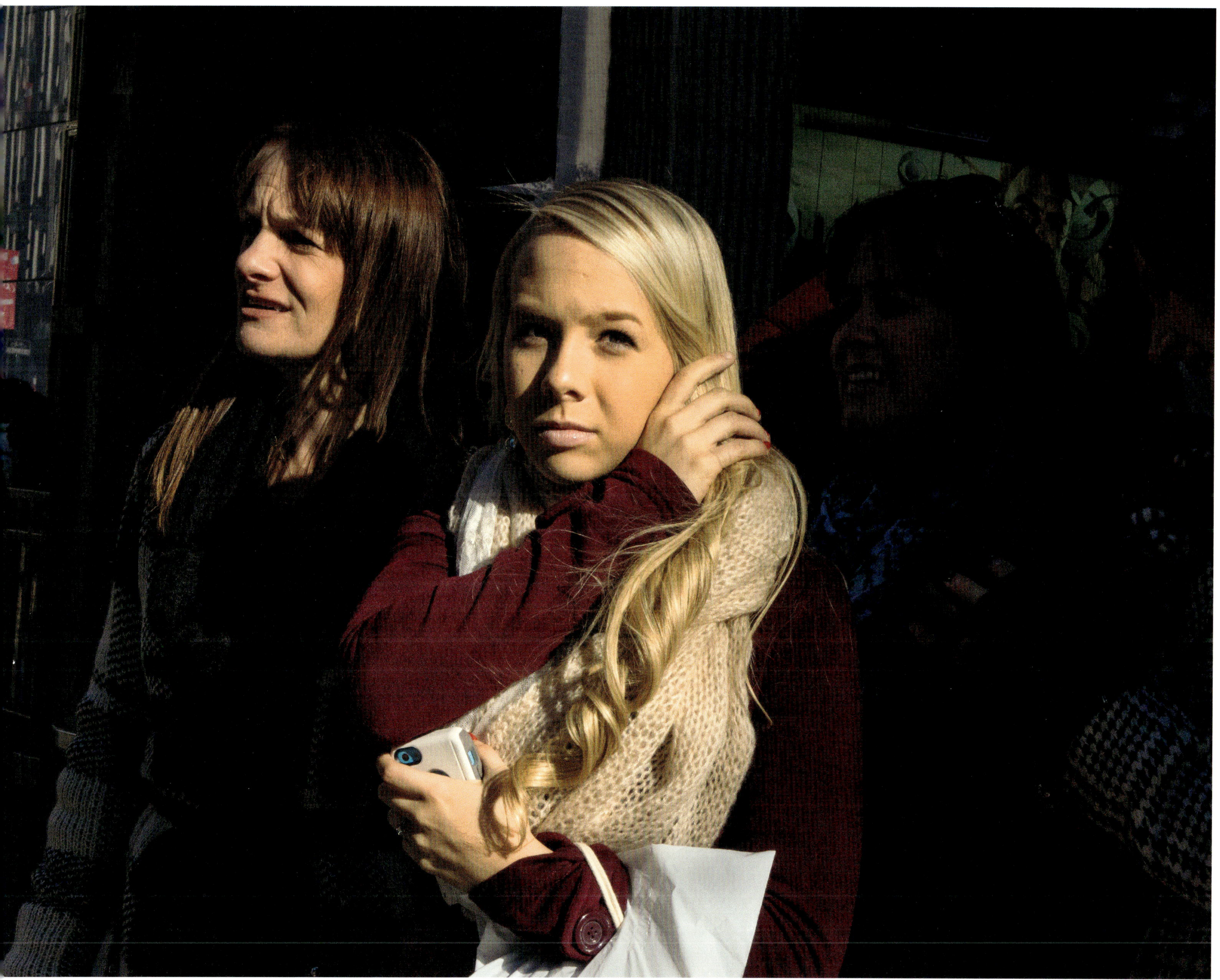

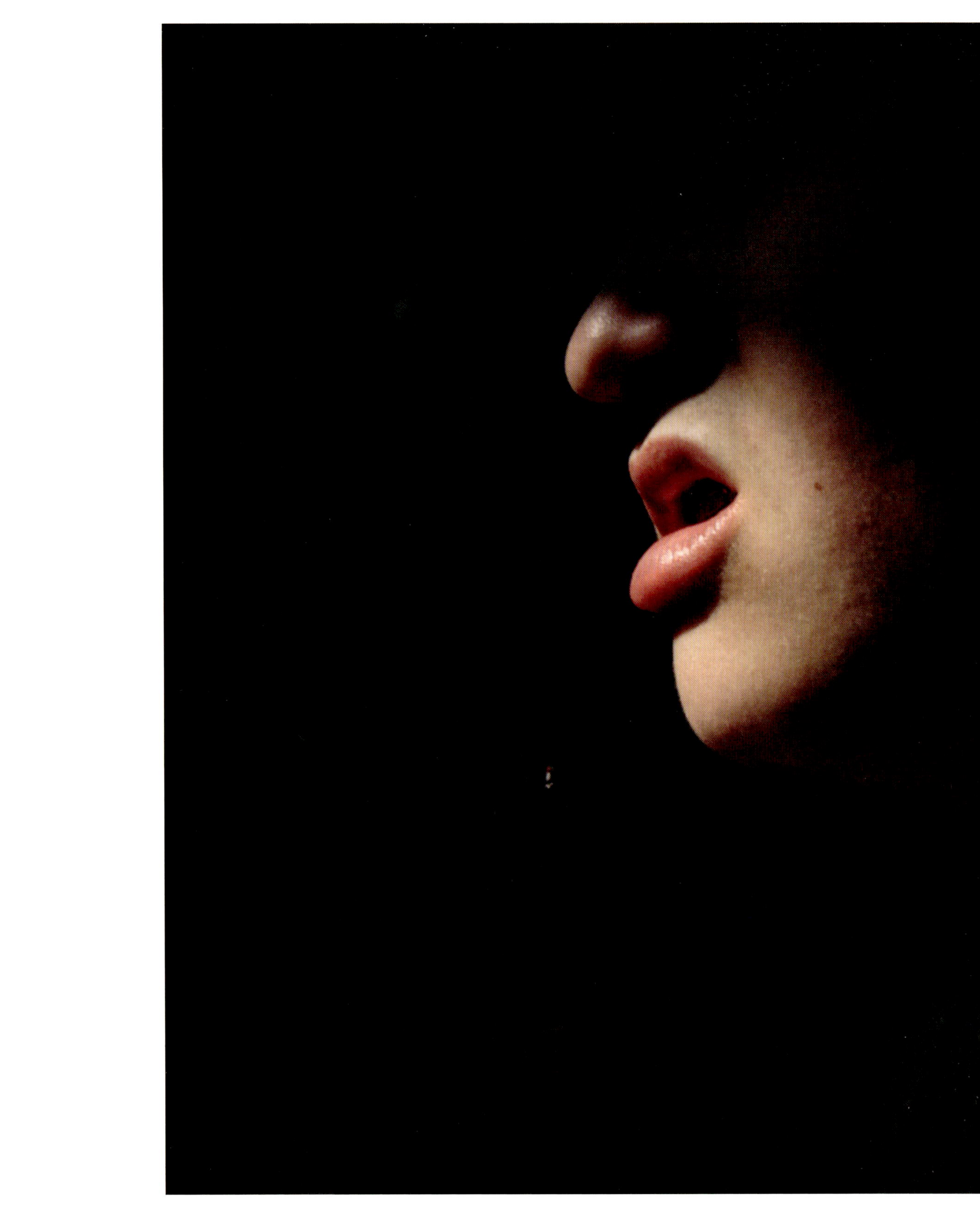

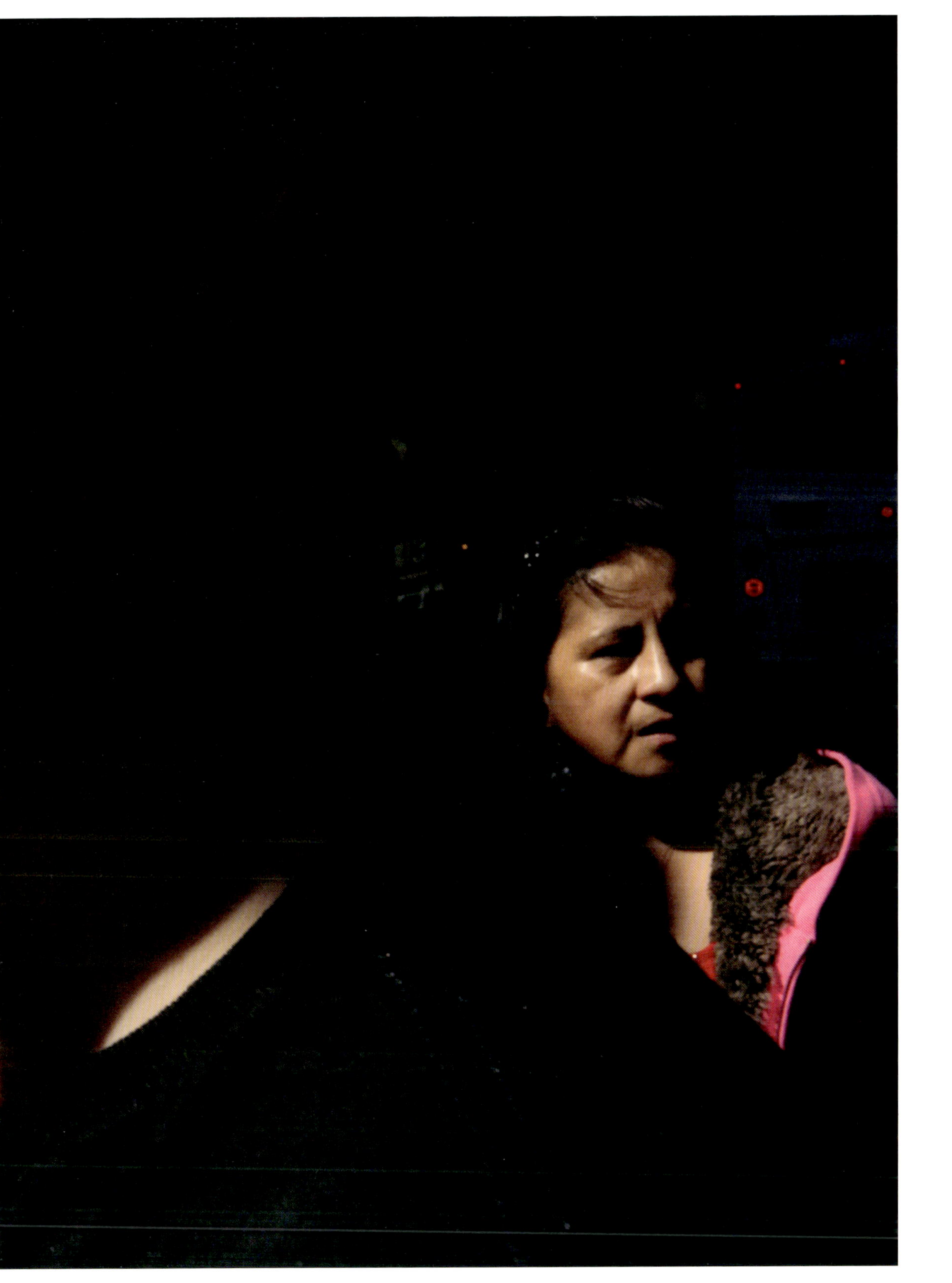

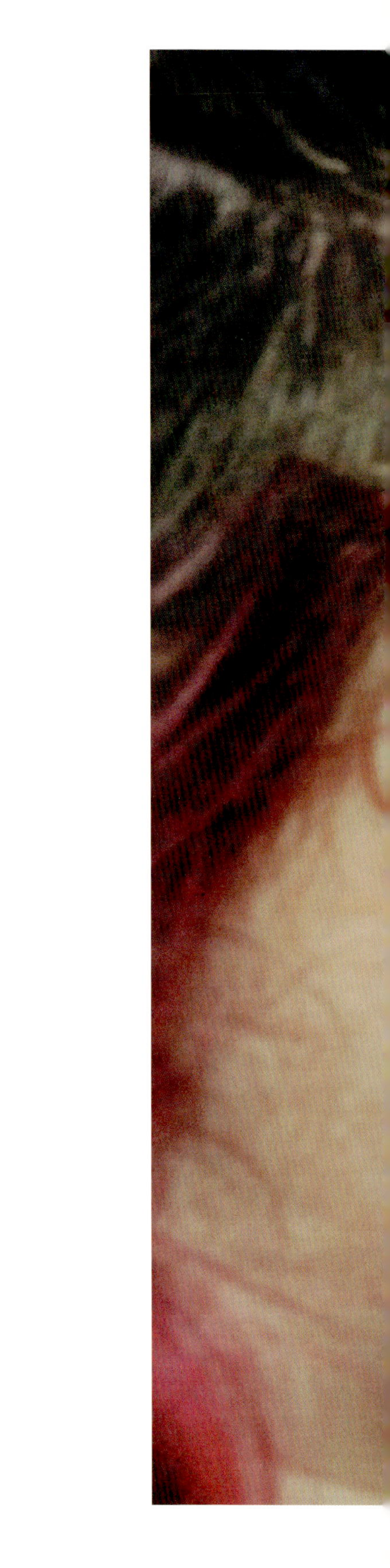

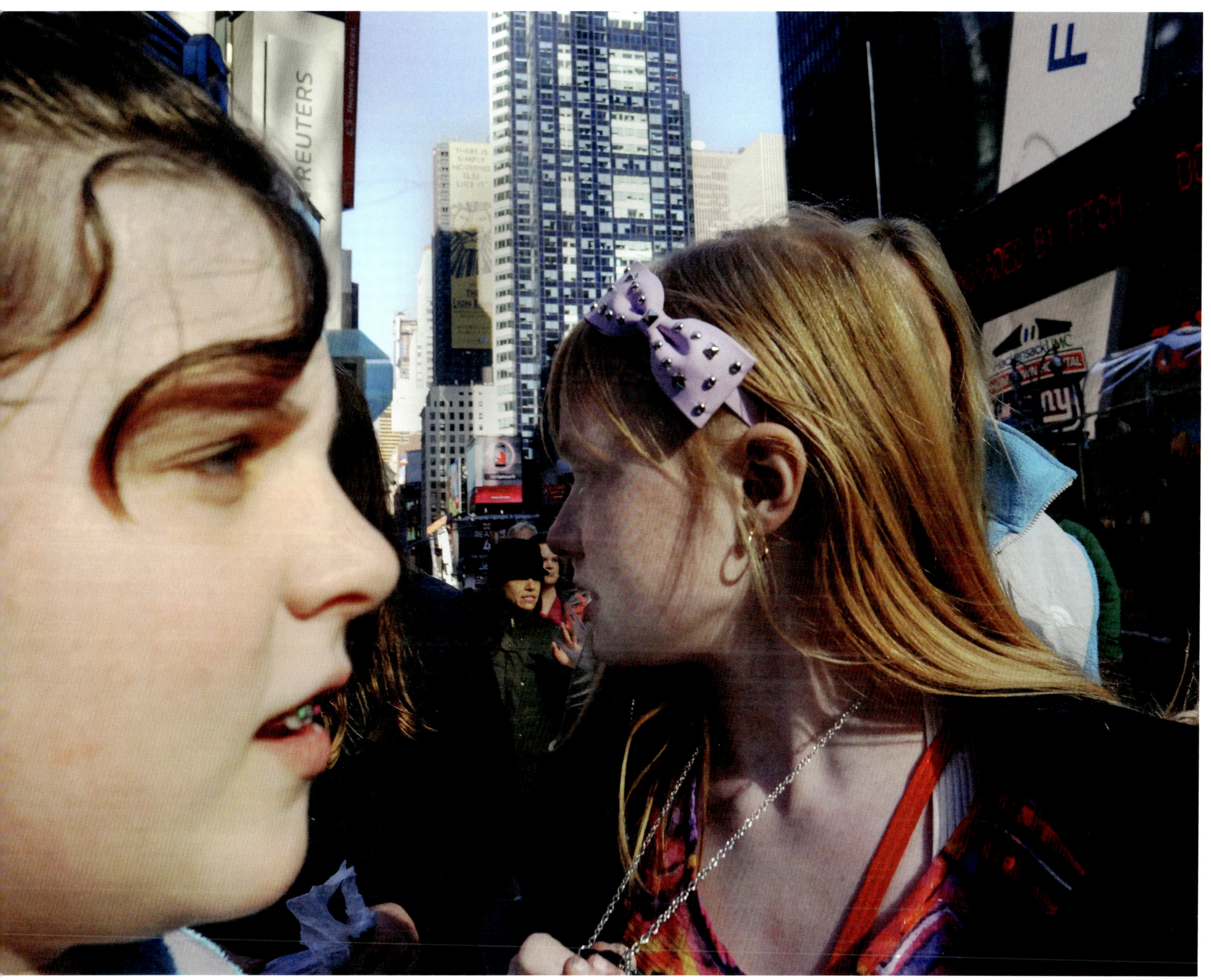
REUTERS
THERE IS
SIMPLY
NOTHING
ELSE
LIKE IT.
F

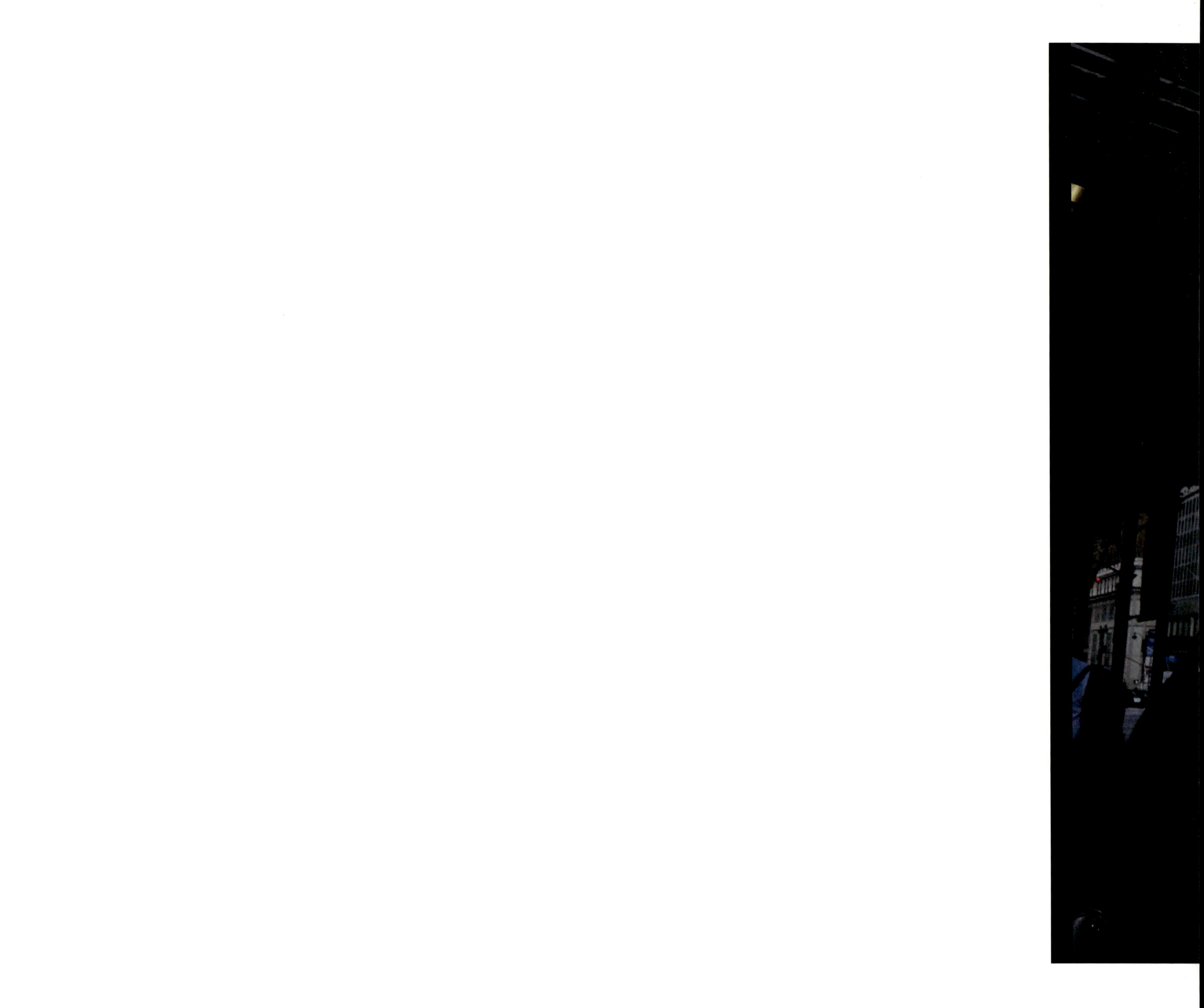

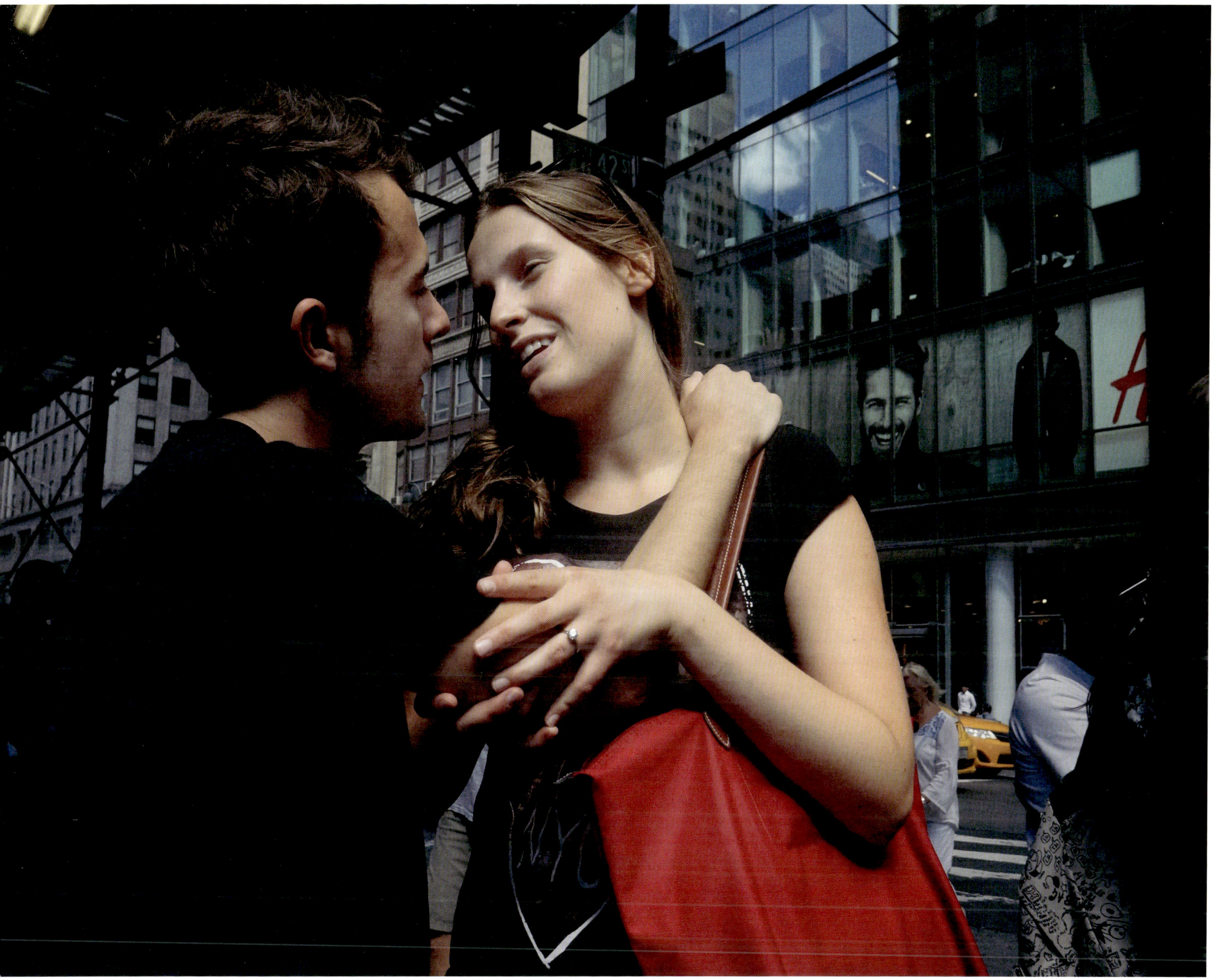

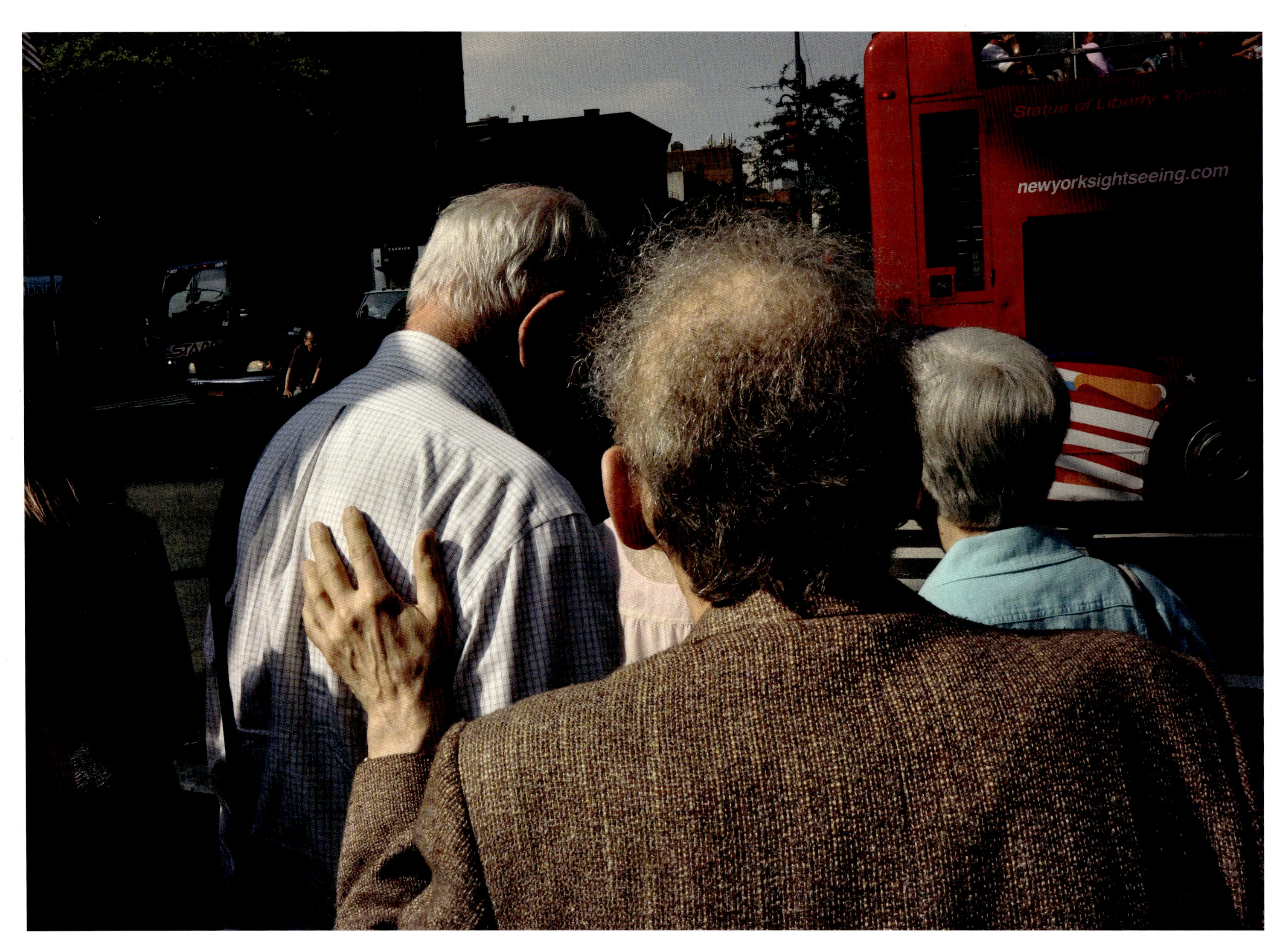

Statue of Liberty • Times
newyorksightseeing.com

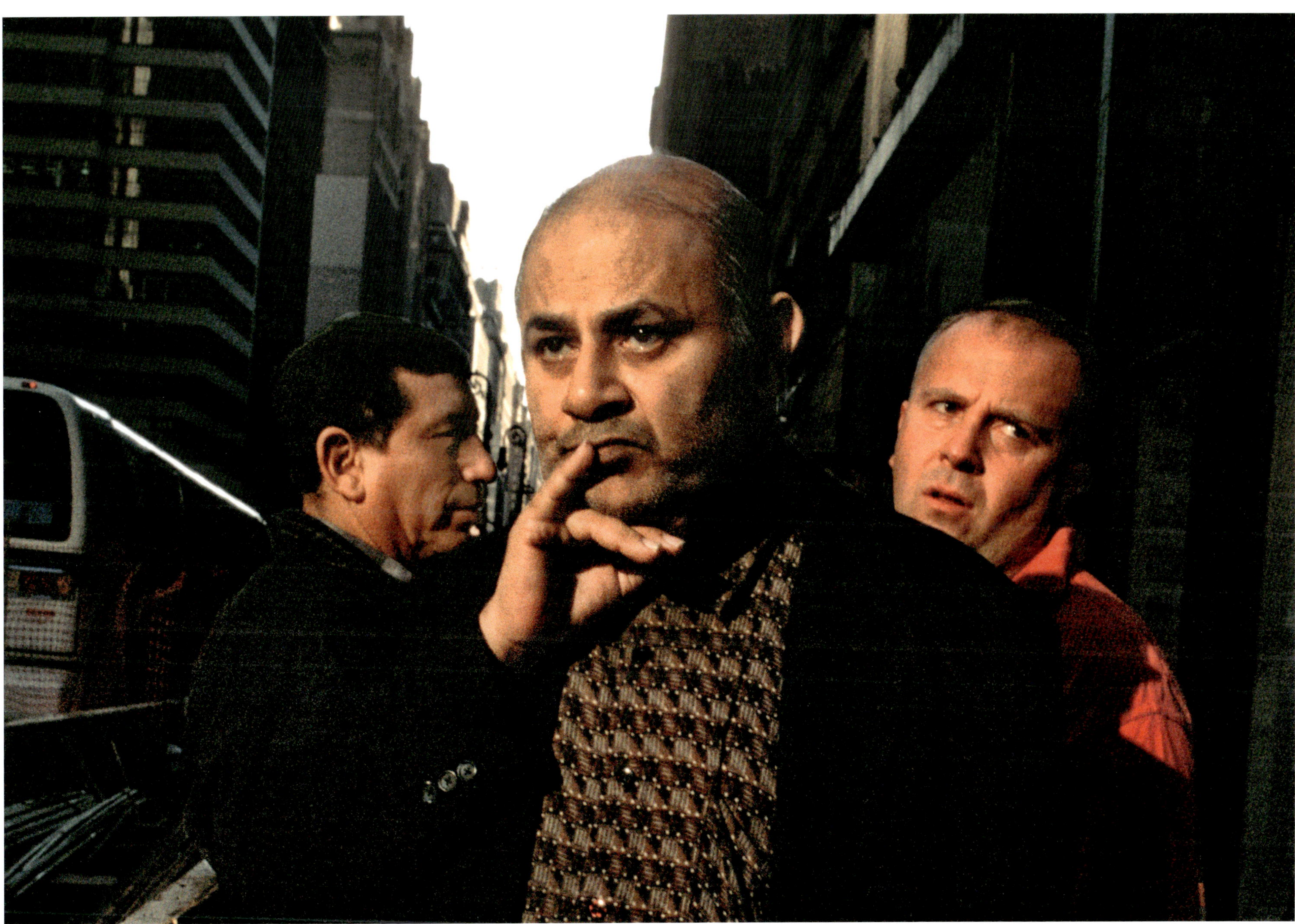

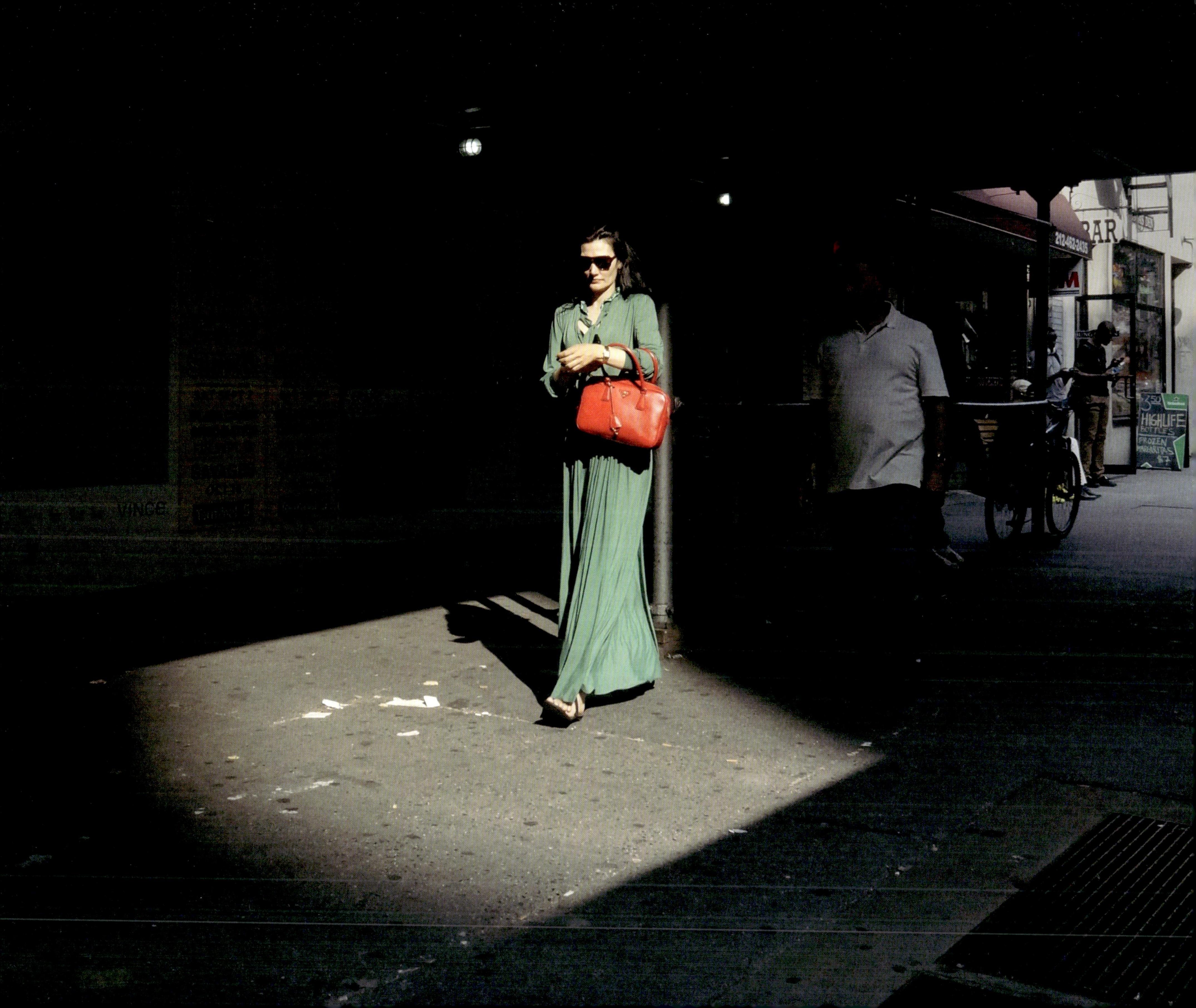

BAR
212-462-3435
3.50
HIGHLIFE
BOTTLES
FROZEN
MARGARITAS
$7

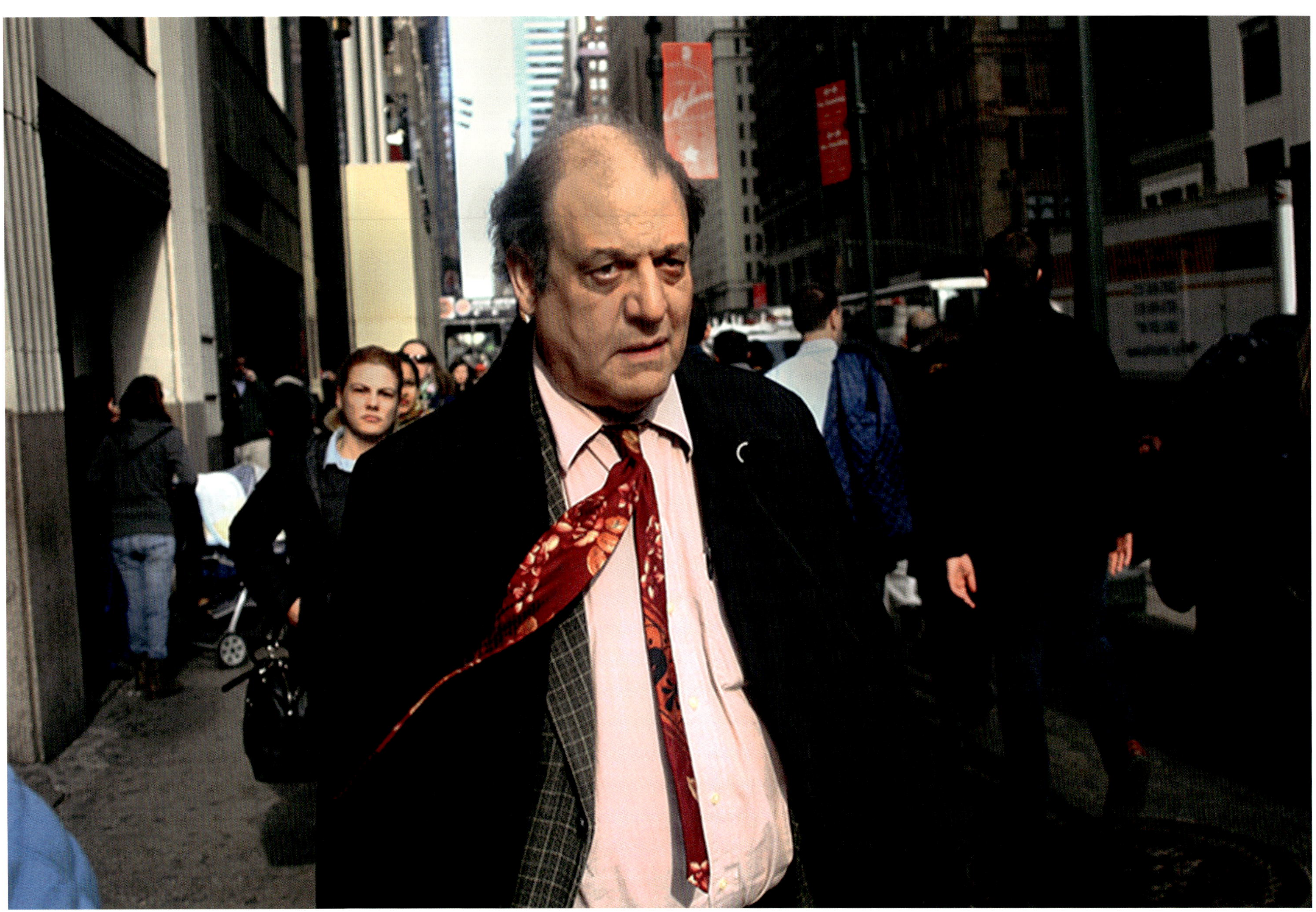

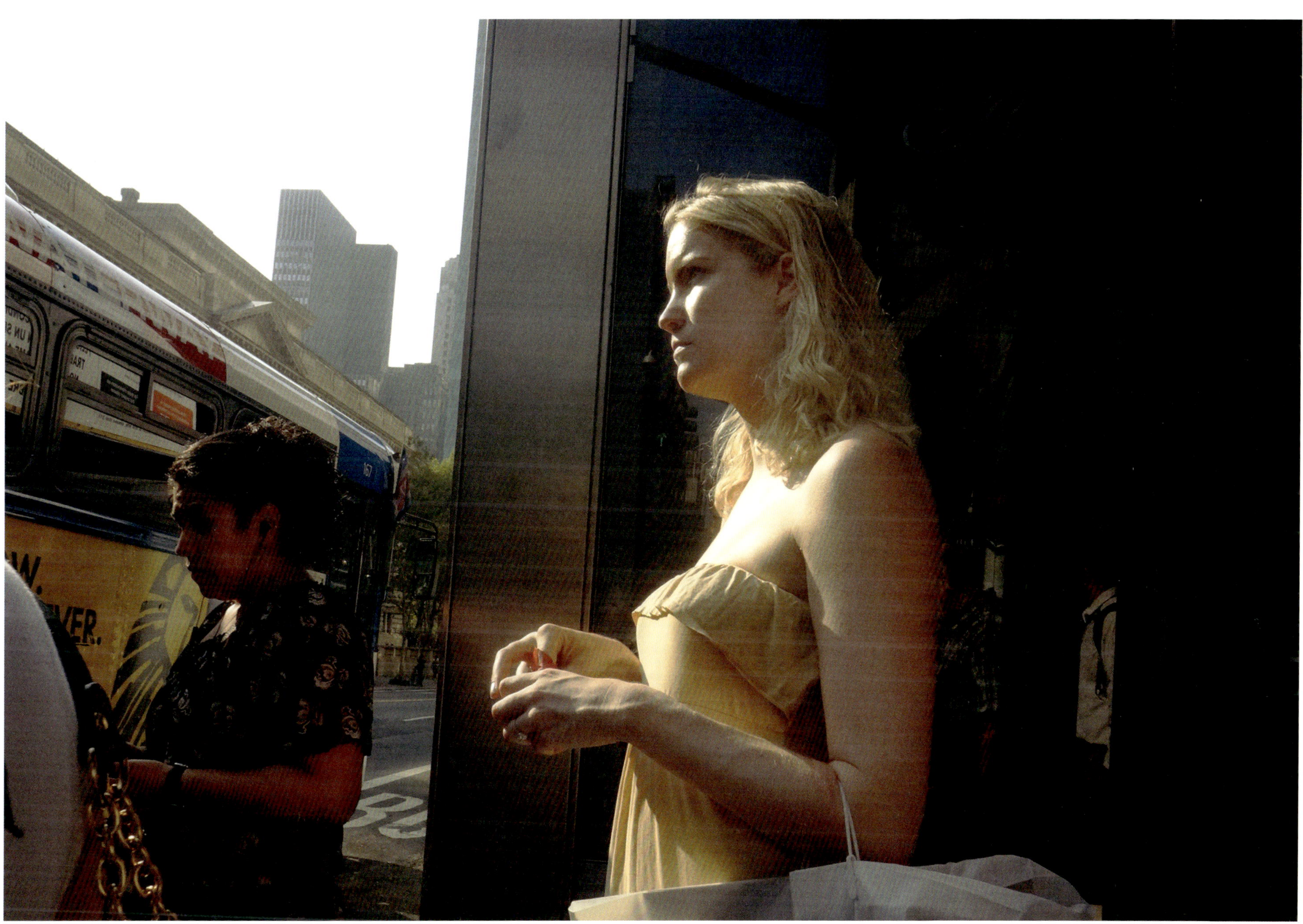

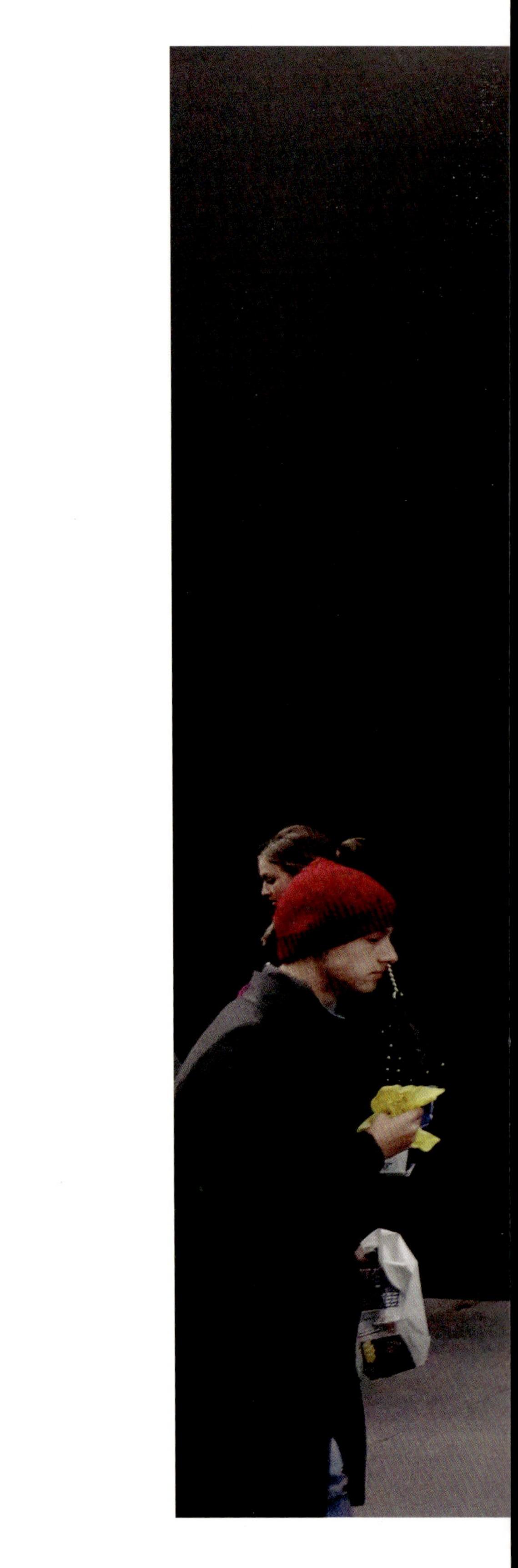

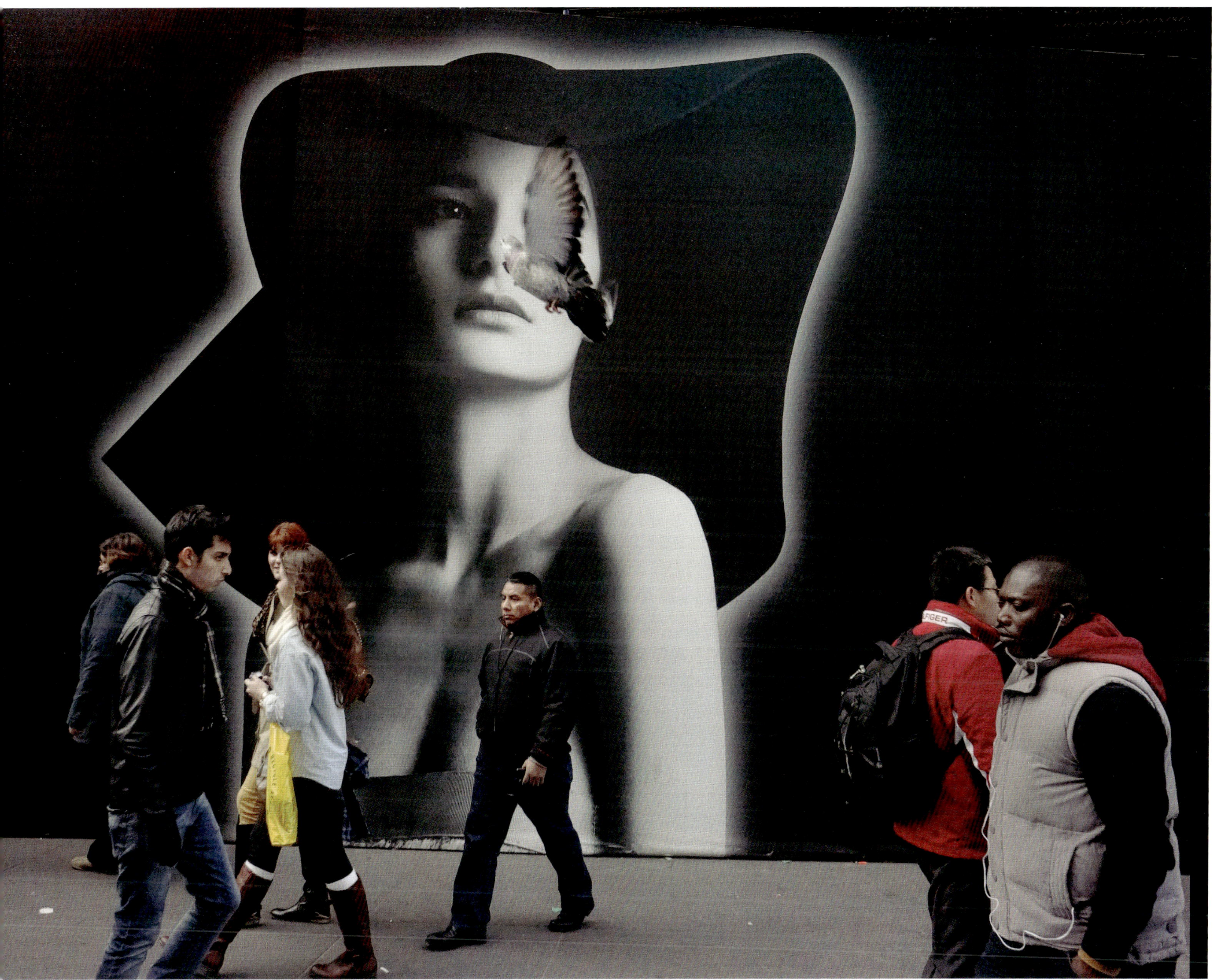

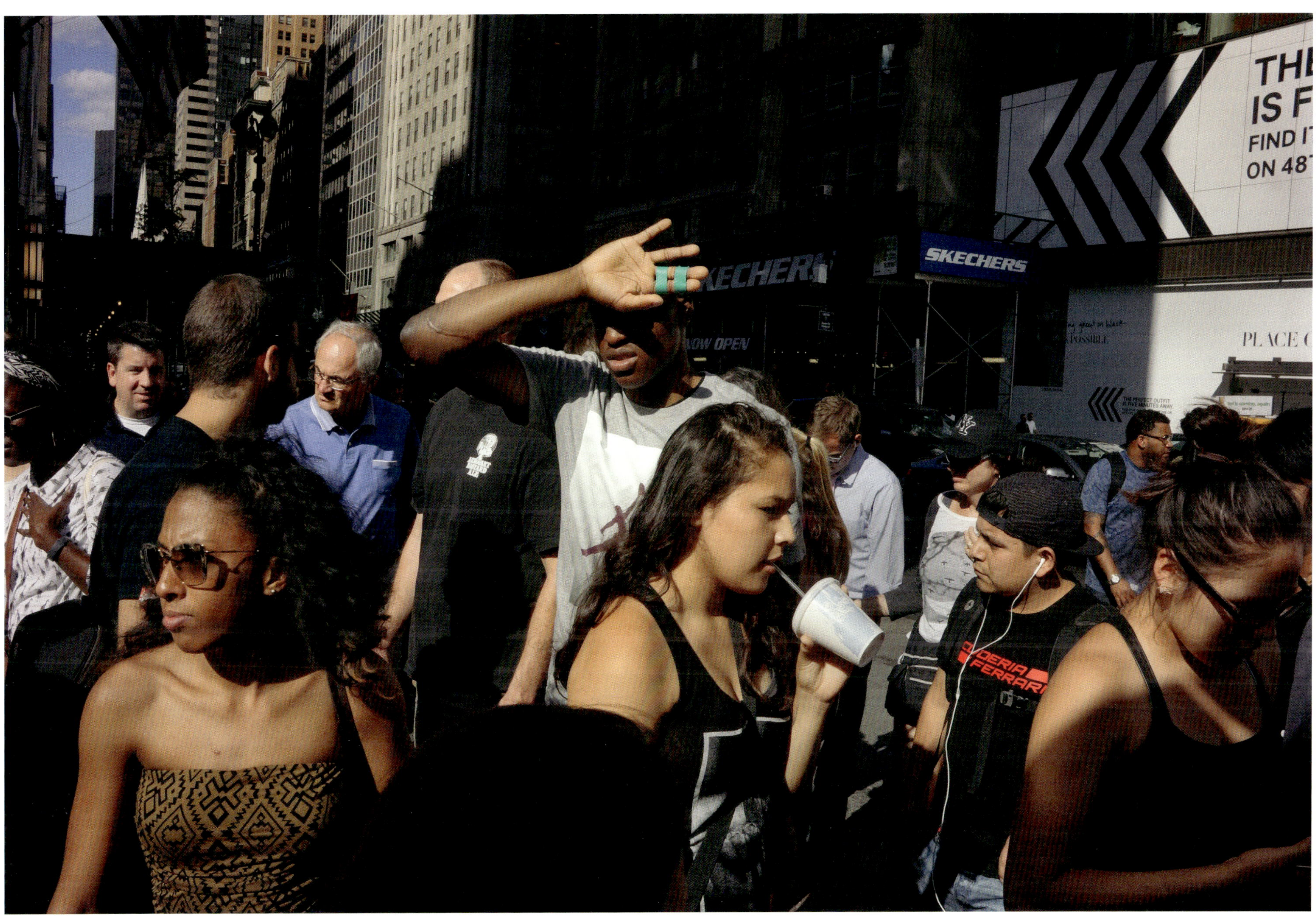
SKECHERS
SKECHERS
THE
IS F
FIND IT
ON 48
NOW OPEN
PLACE
THE PERFECT OUTFIT
IS FIVE MINUTES AWAY
FERRARI

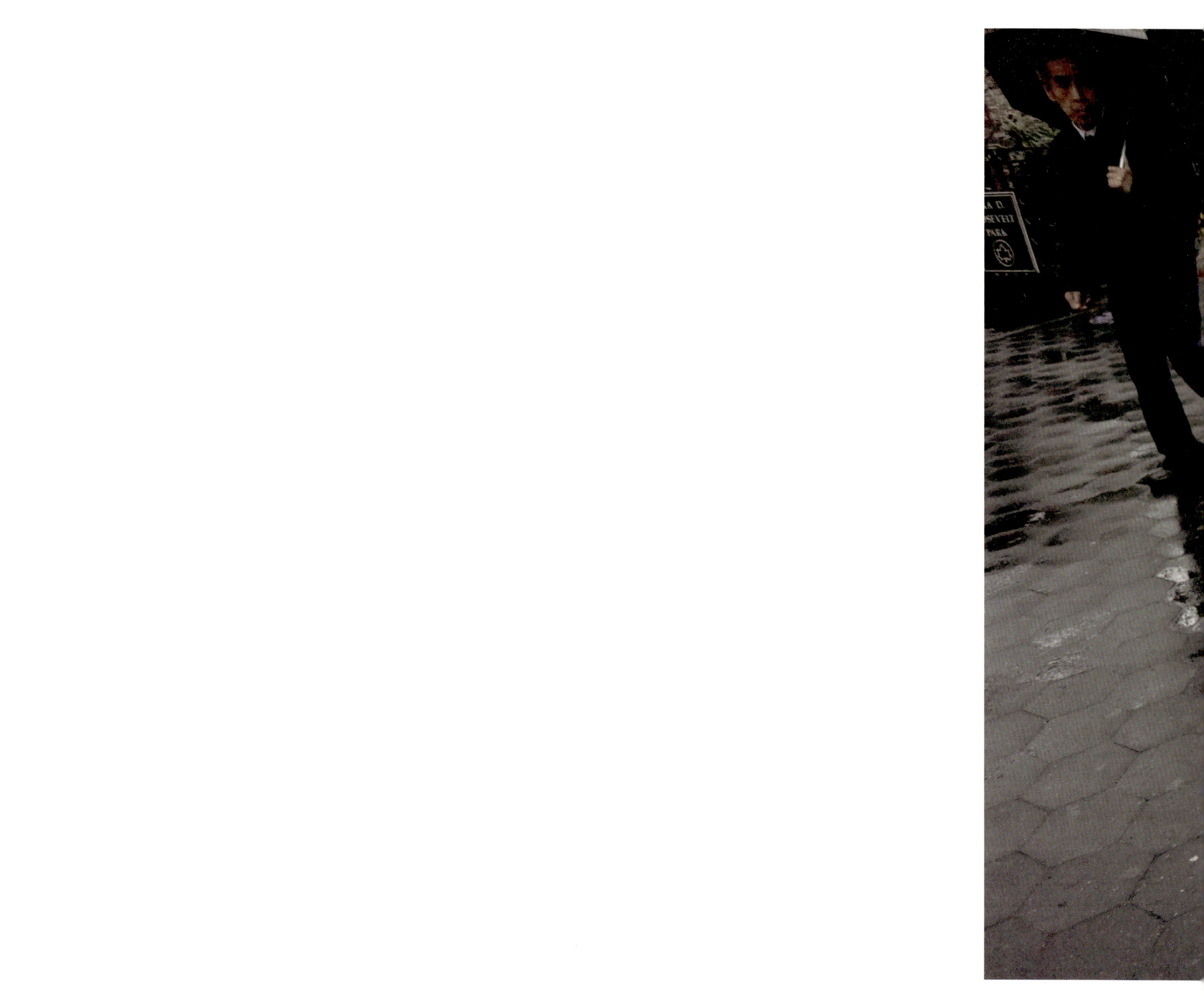
A D.
SEVELT
PARA

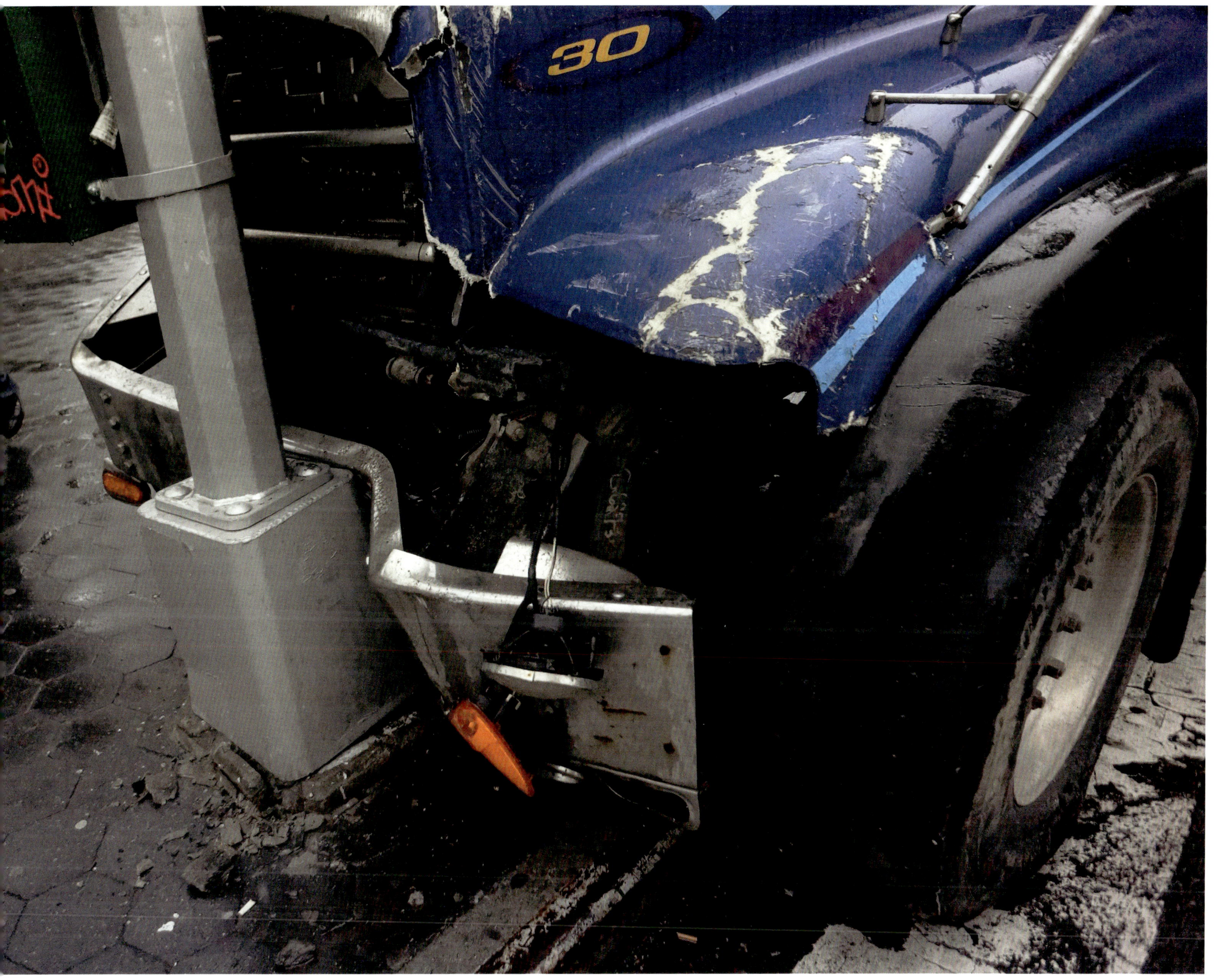

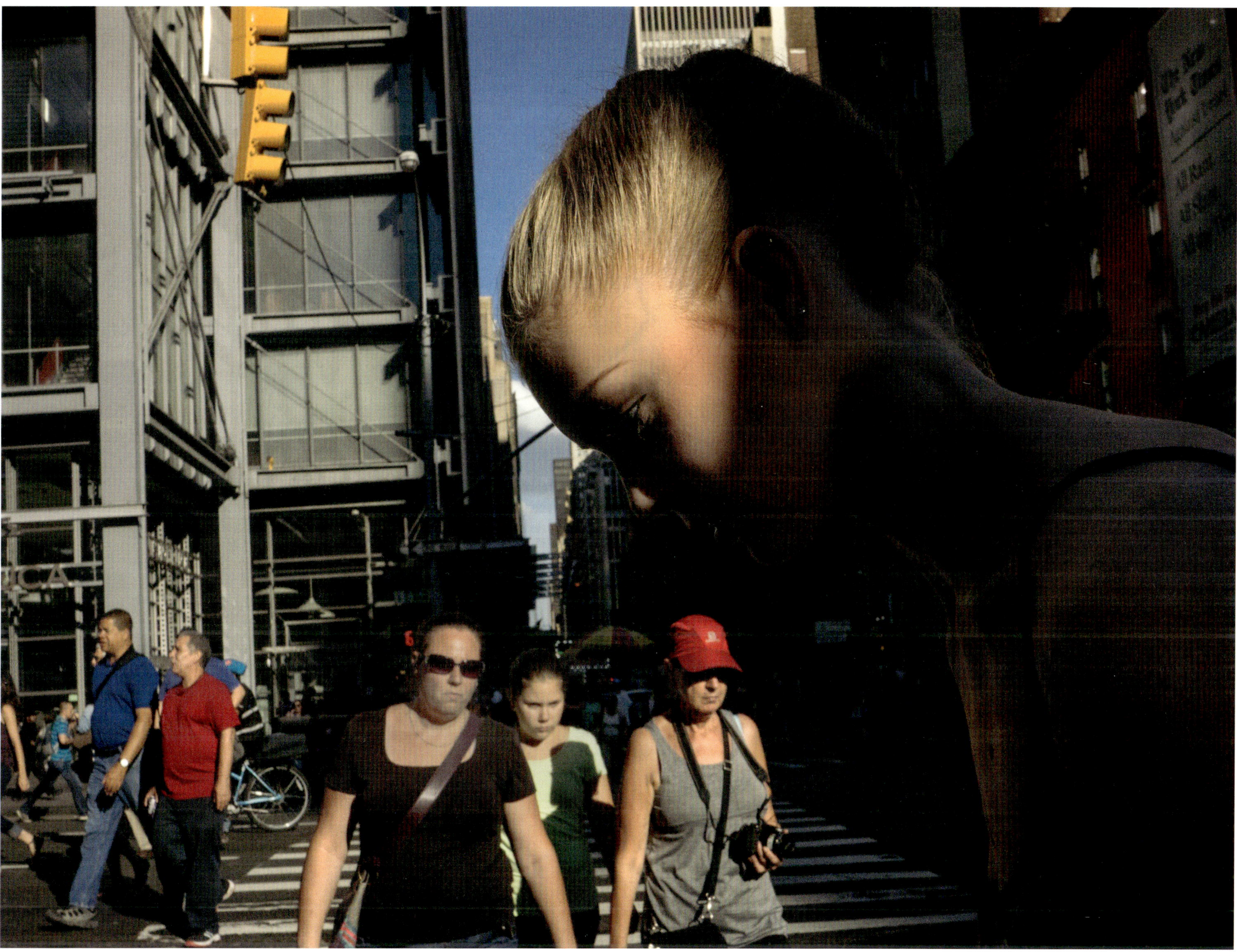

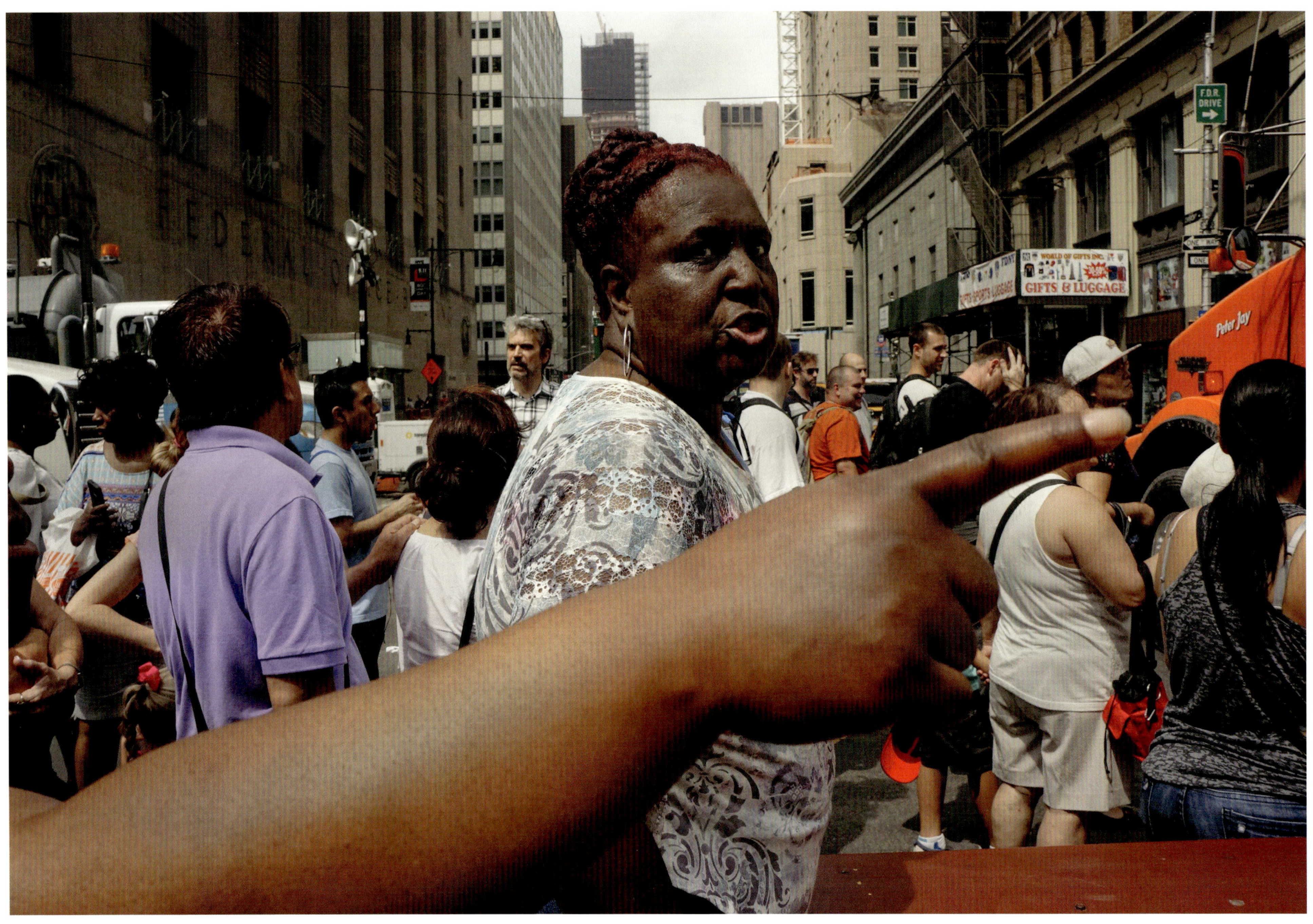

FEDERAL
F.D.R. DRIVE
GIFTS & LUGGAGE
WORLD OF GIFTS INC.
Peter Jay

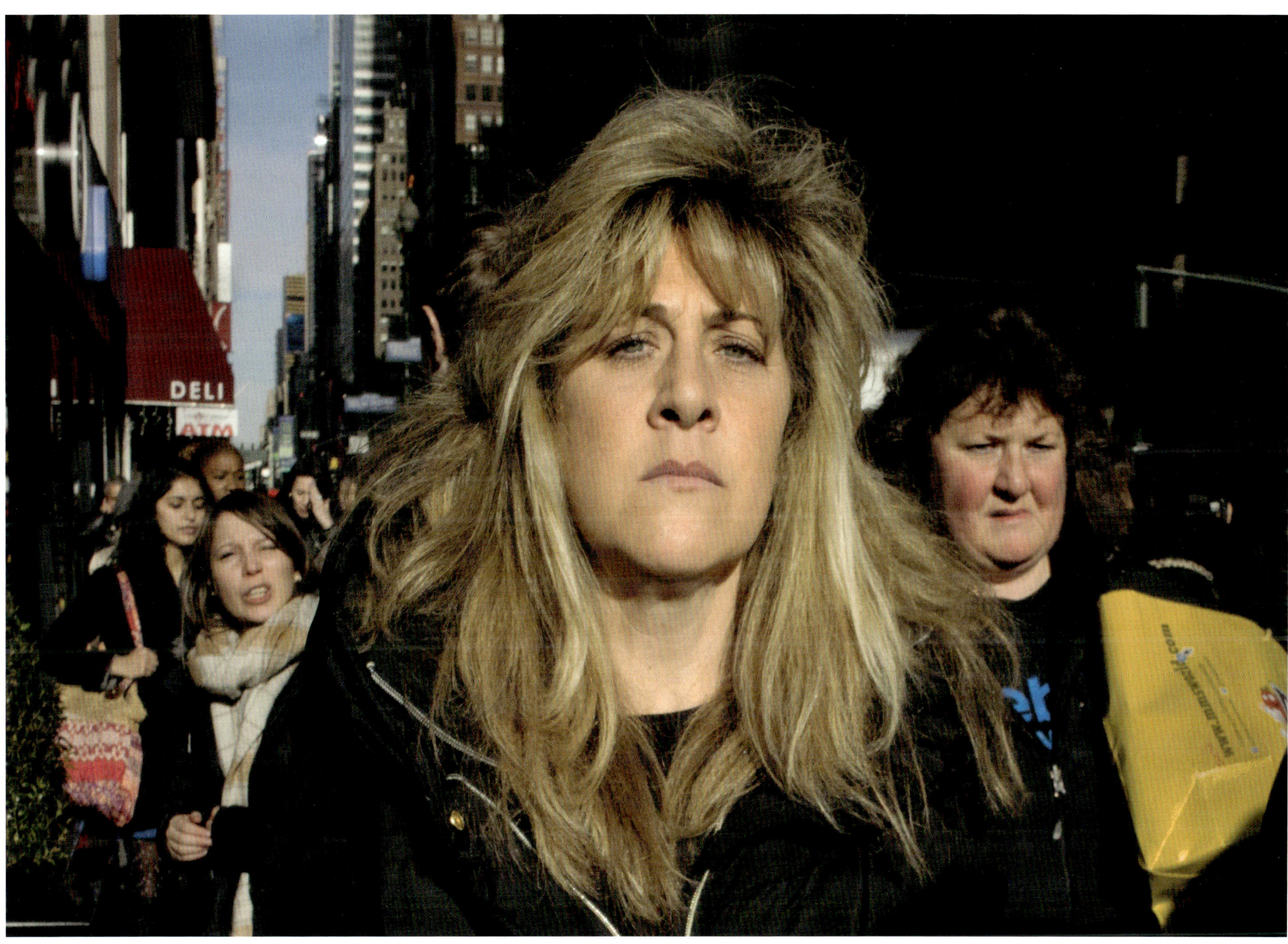

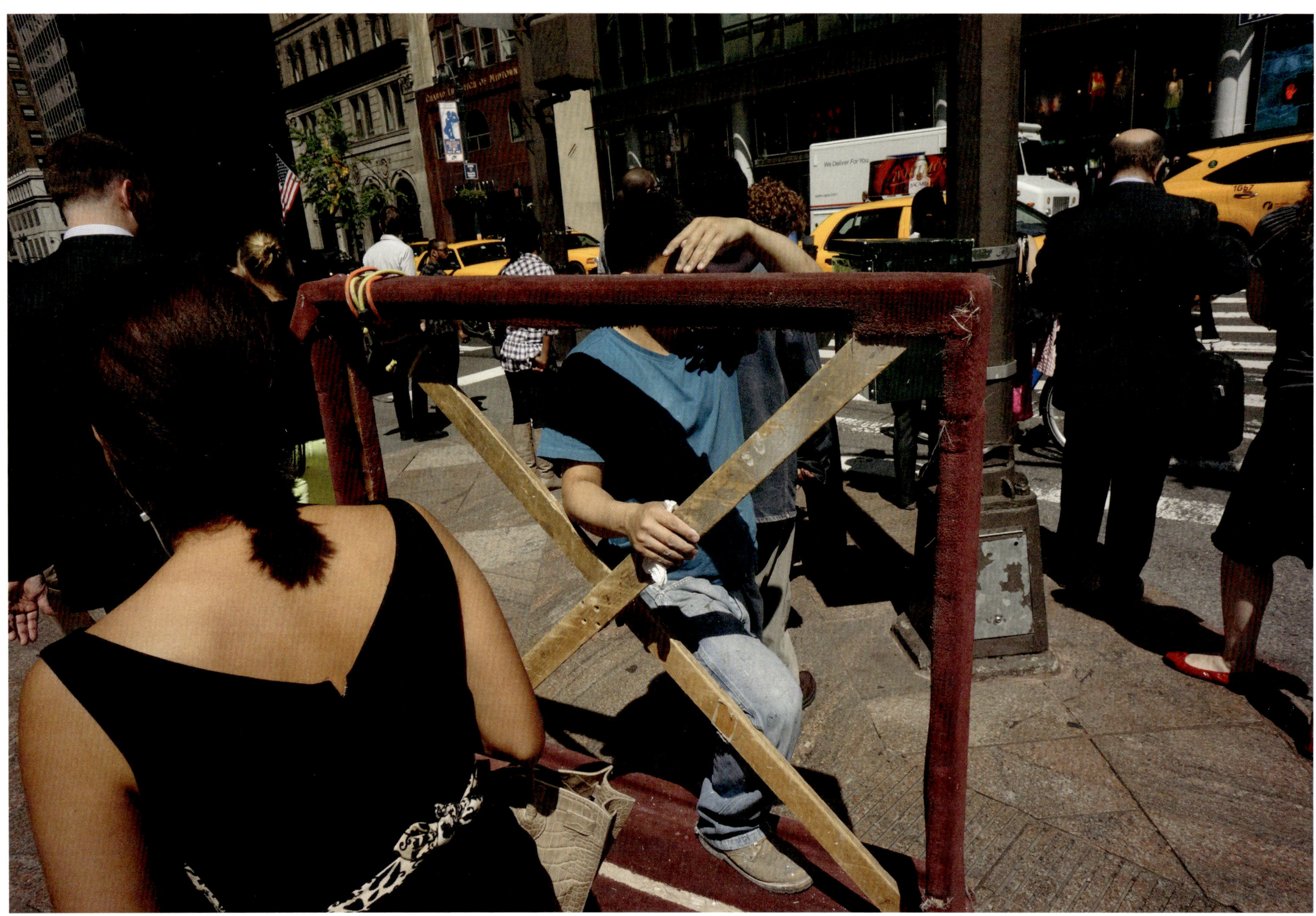

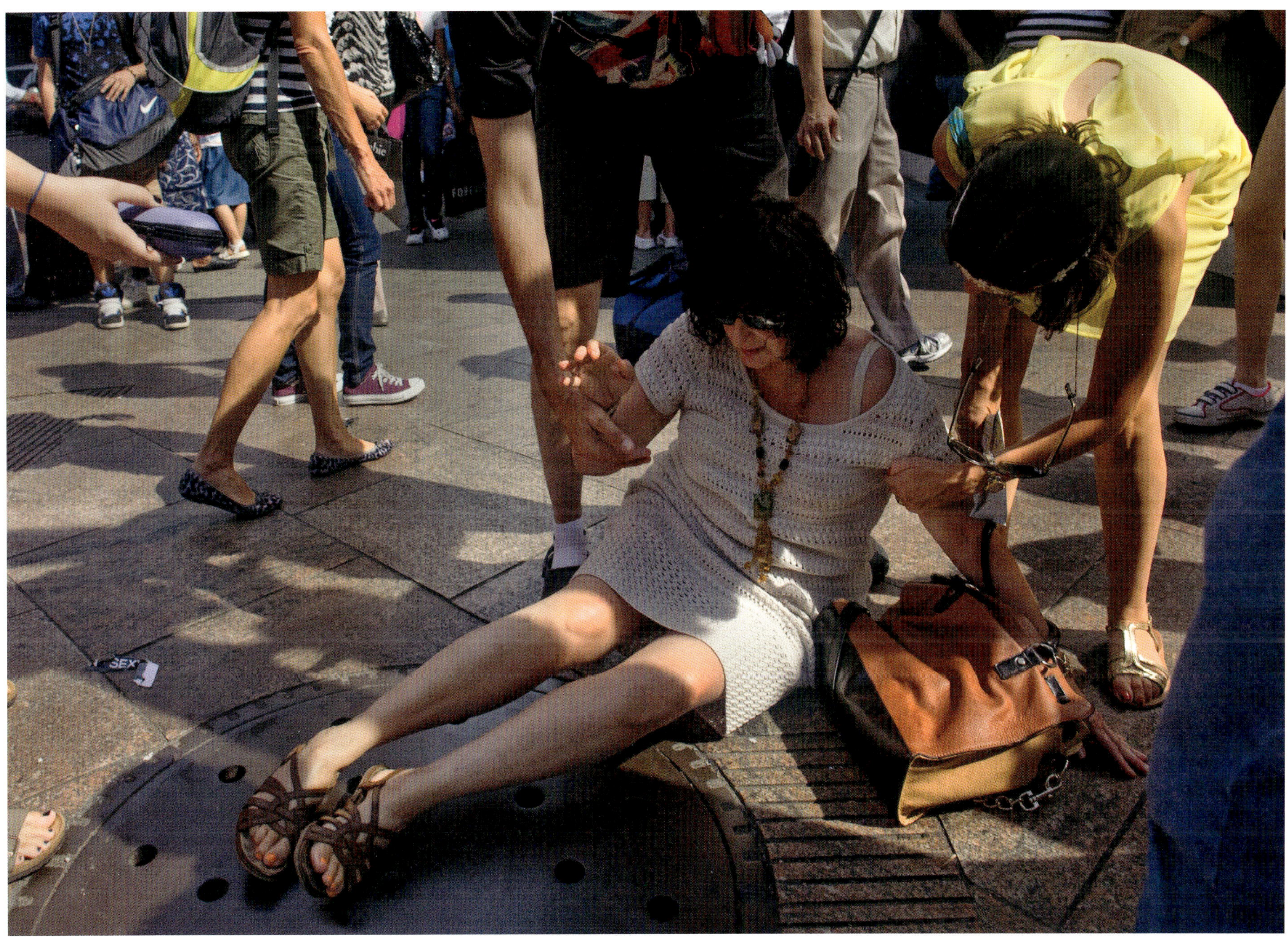

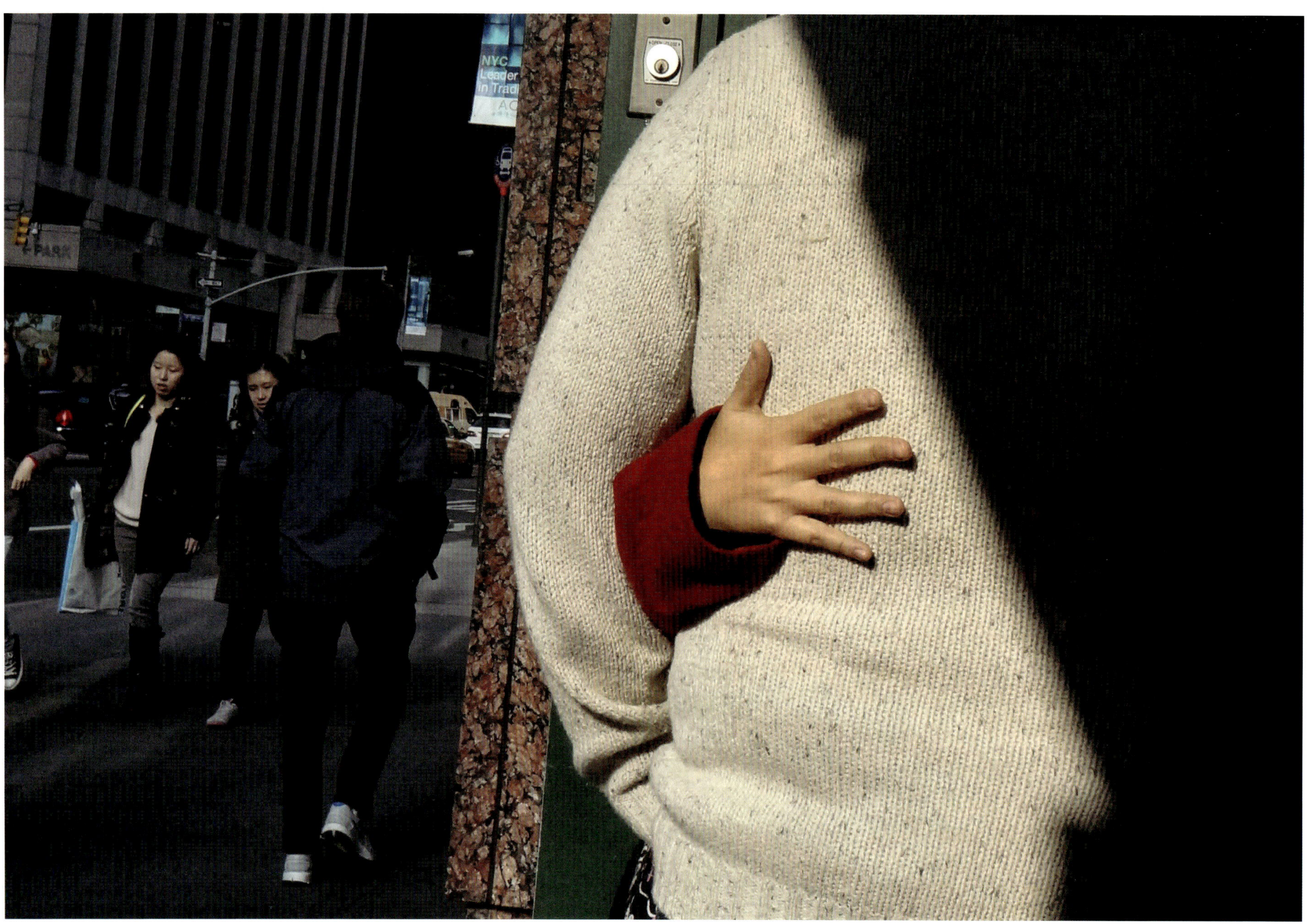

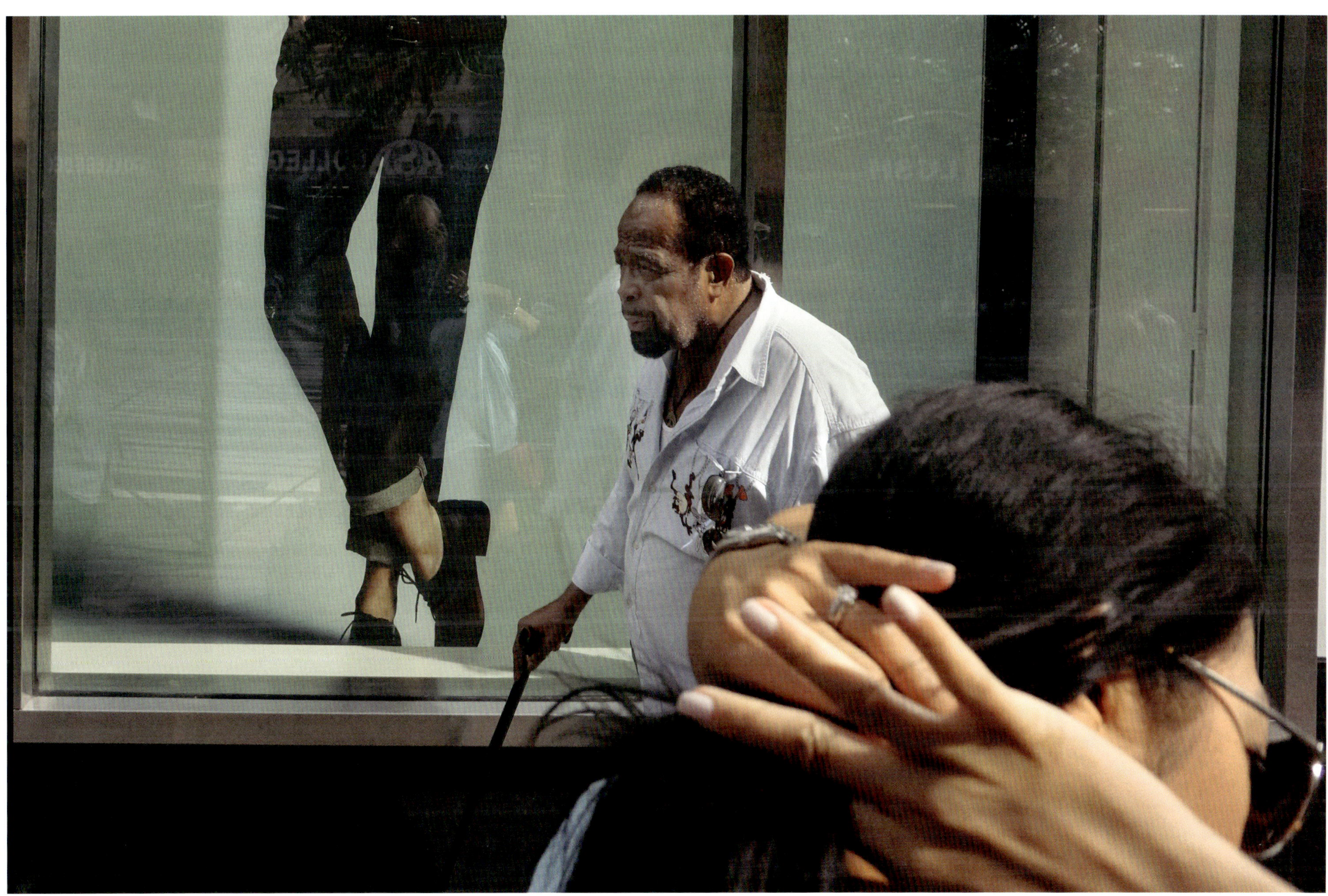

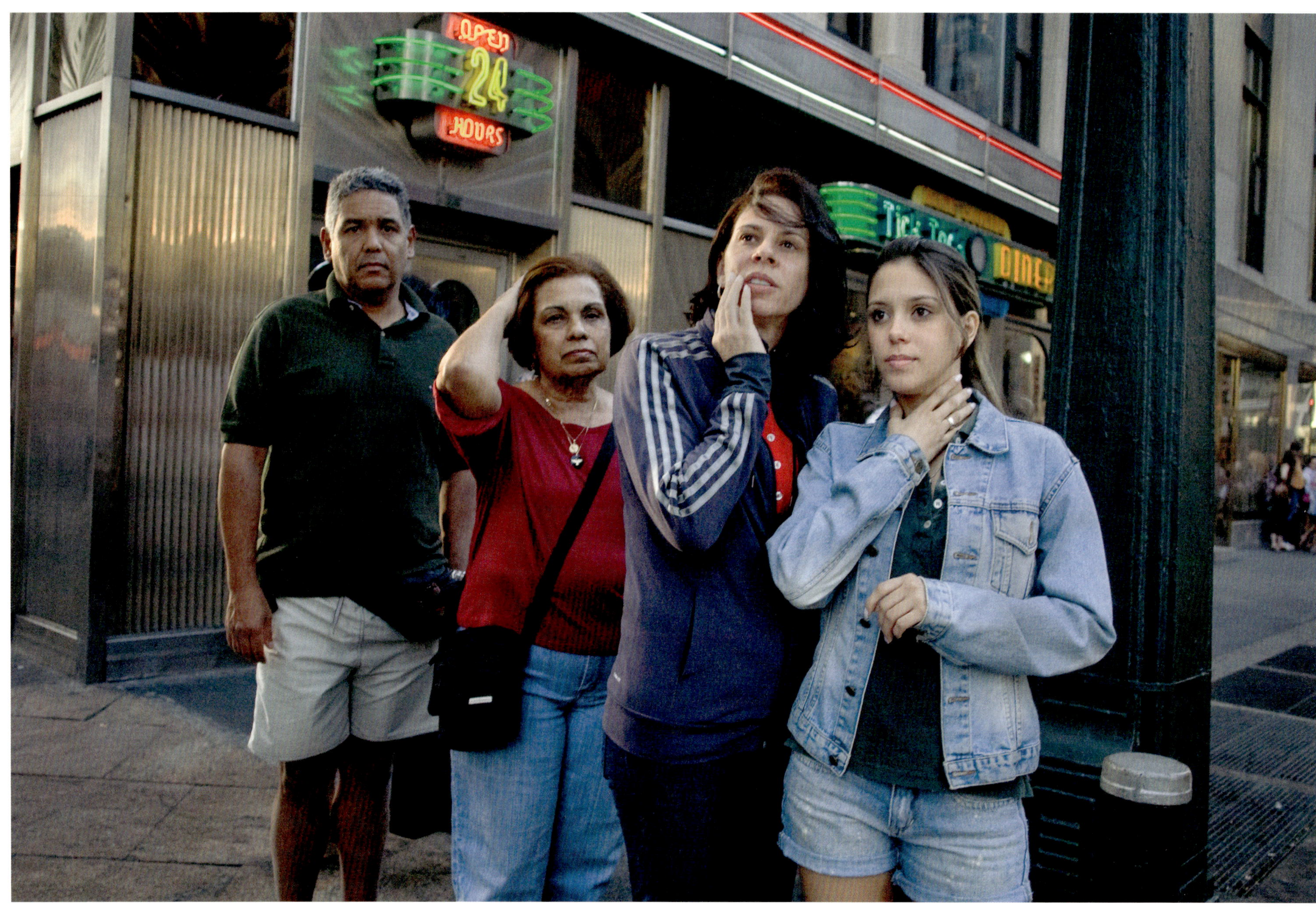

OPEN
24
HOURS
Tick Tock
DINER

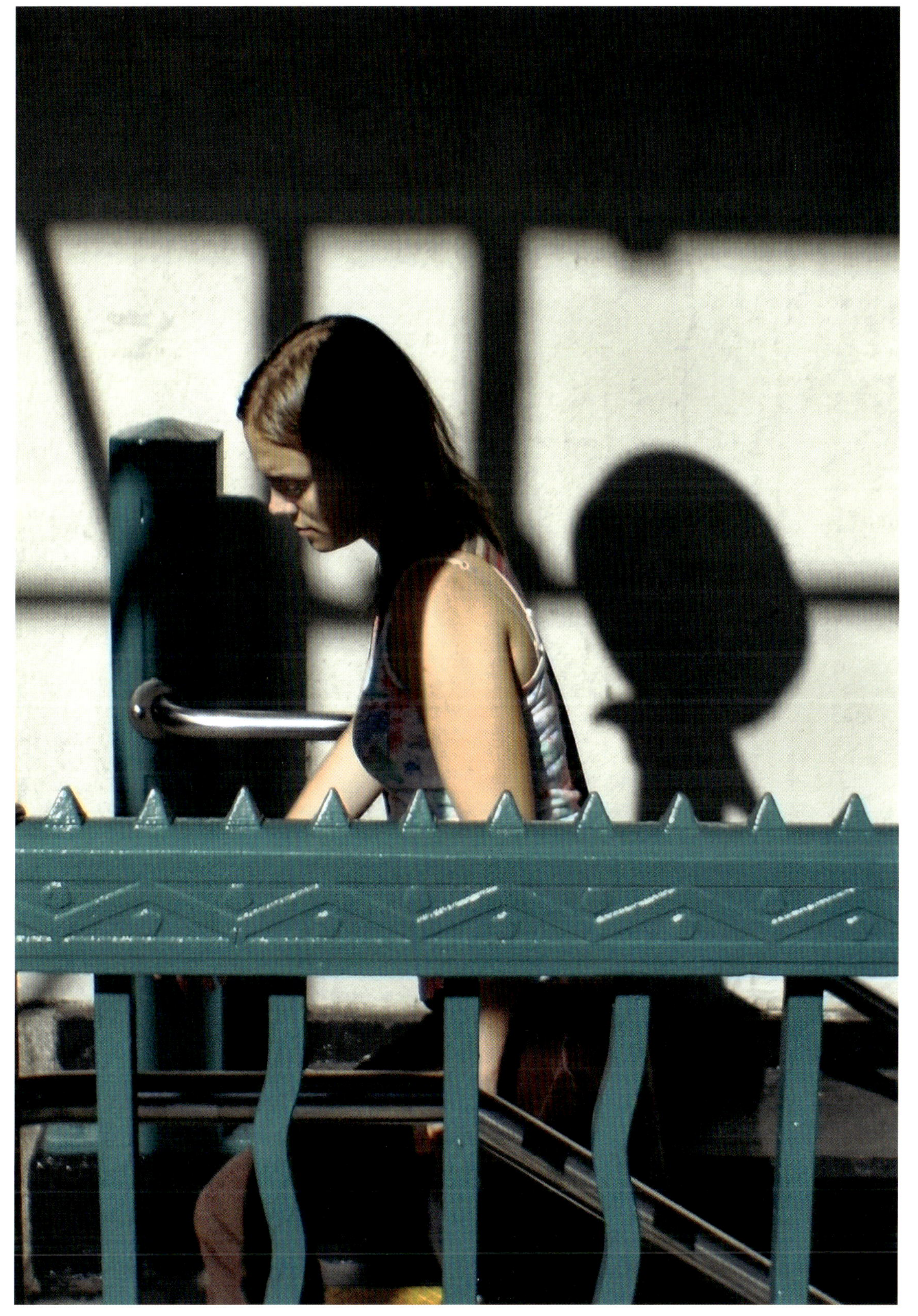

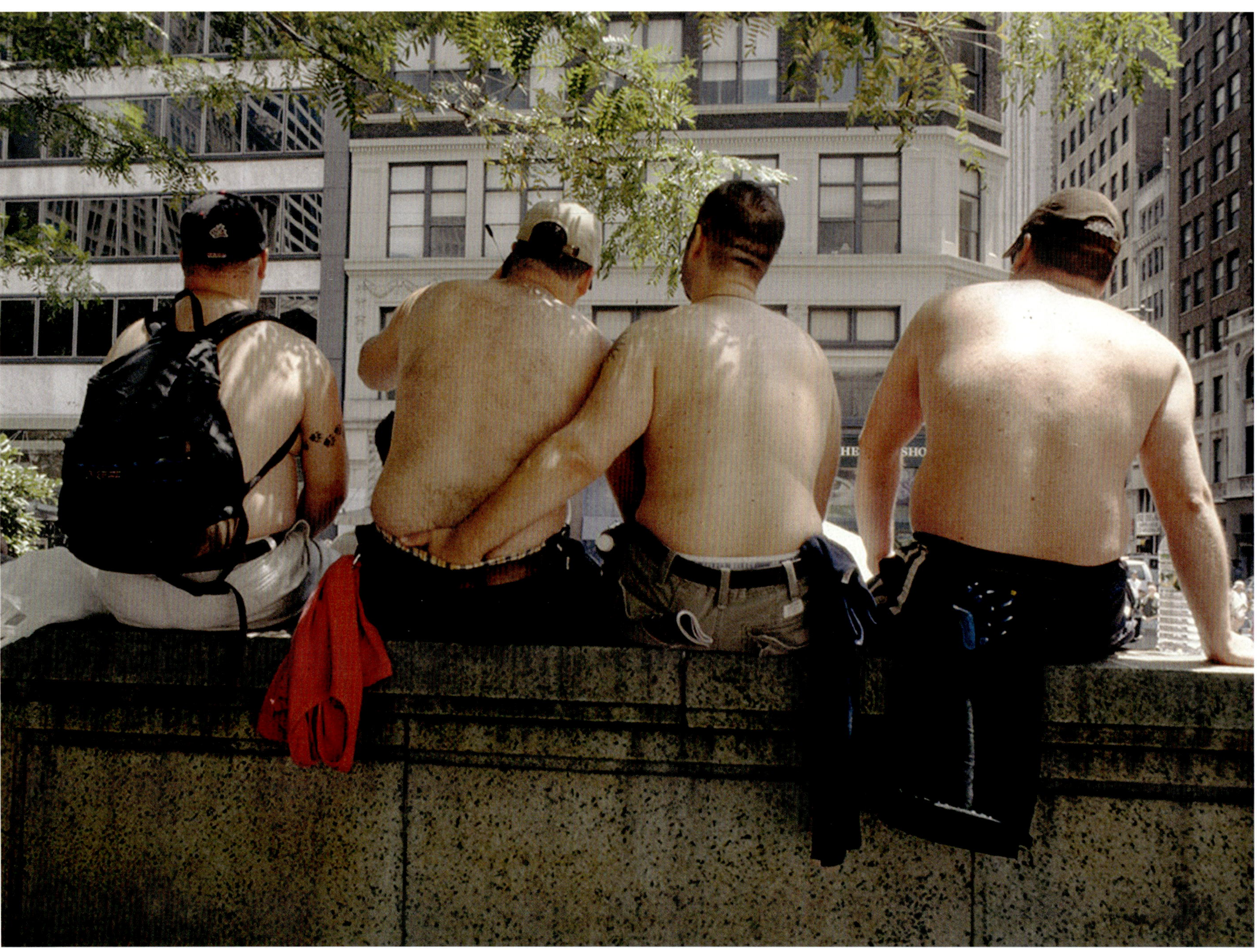

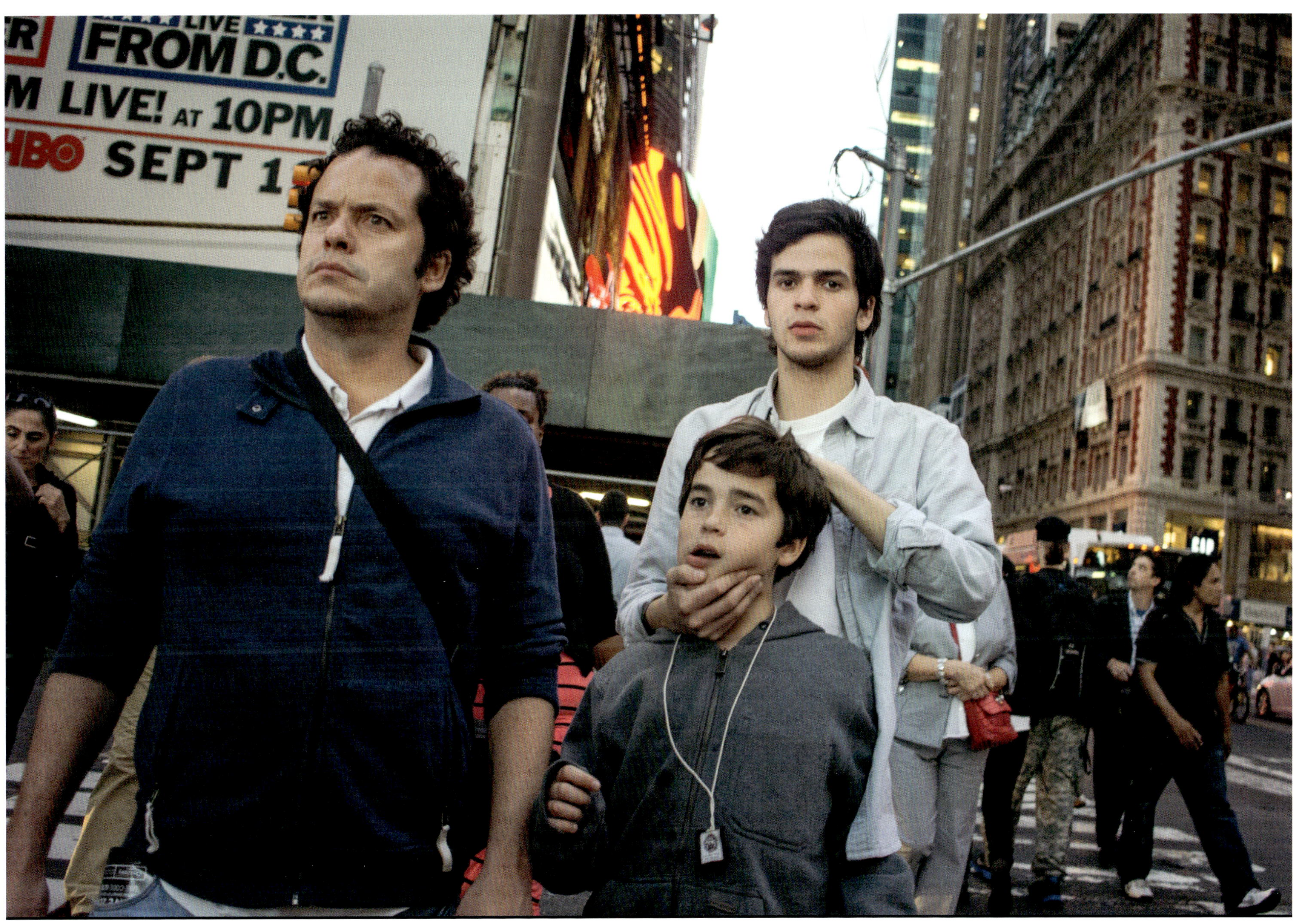
LIVE
FROM D.C.
LIVE! AT 10PM
HBO SEPT 1

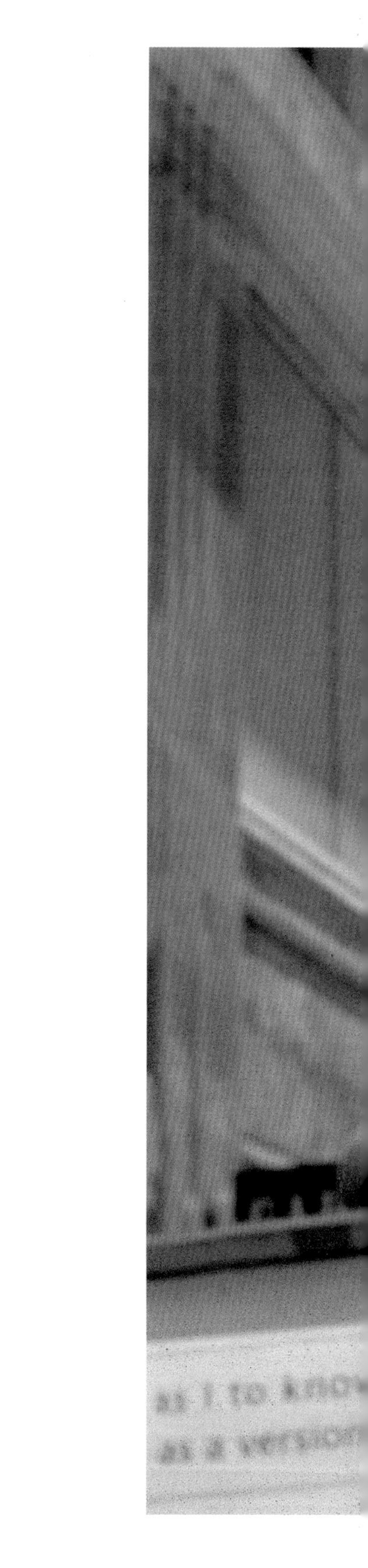

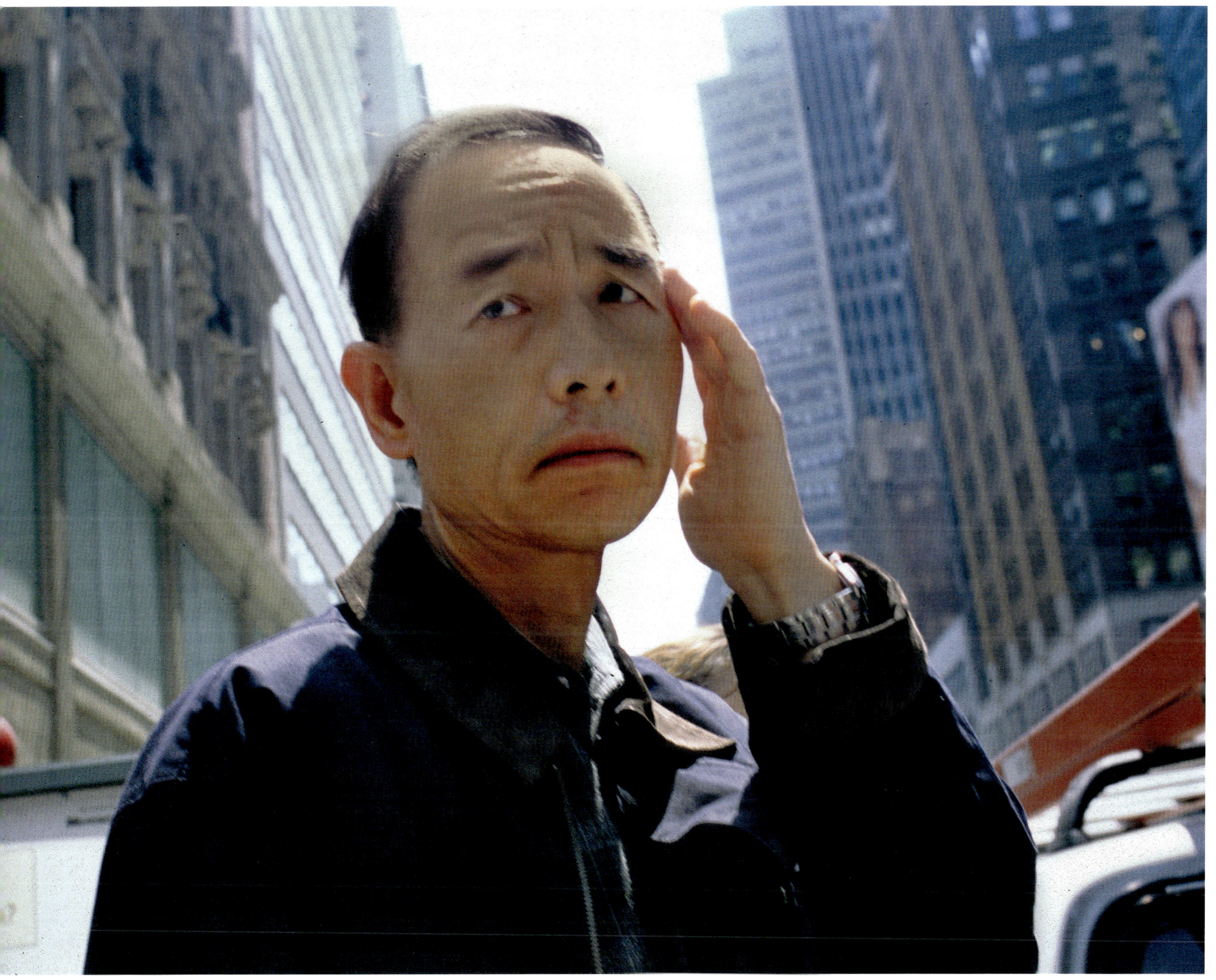

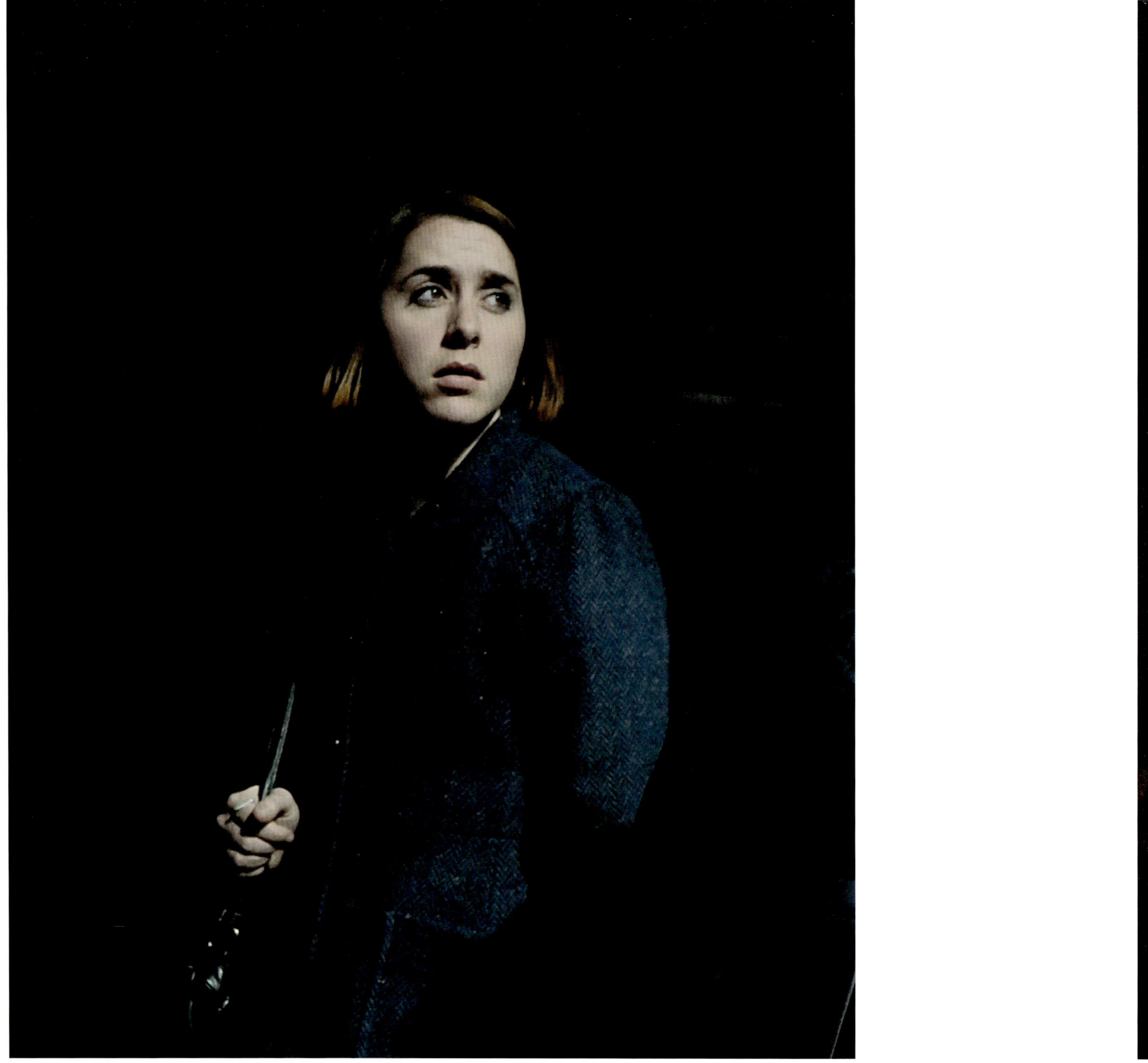

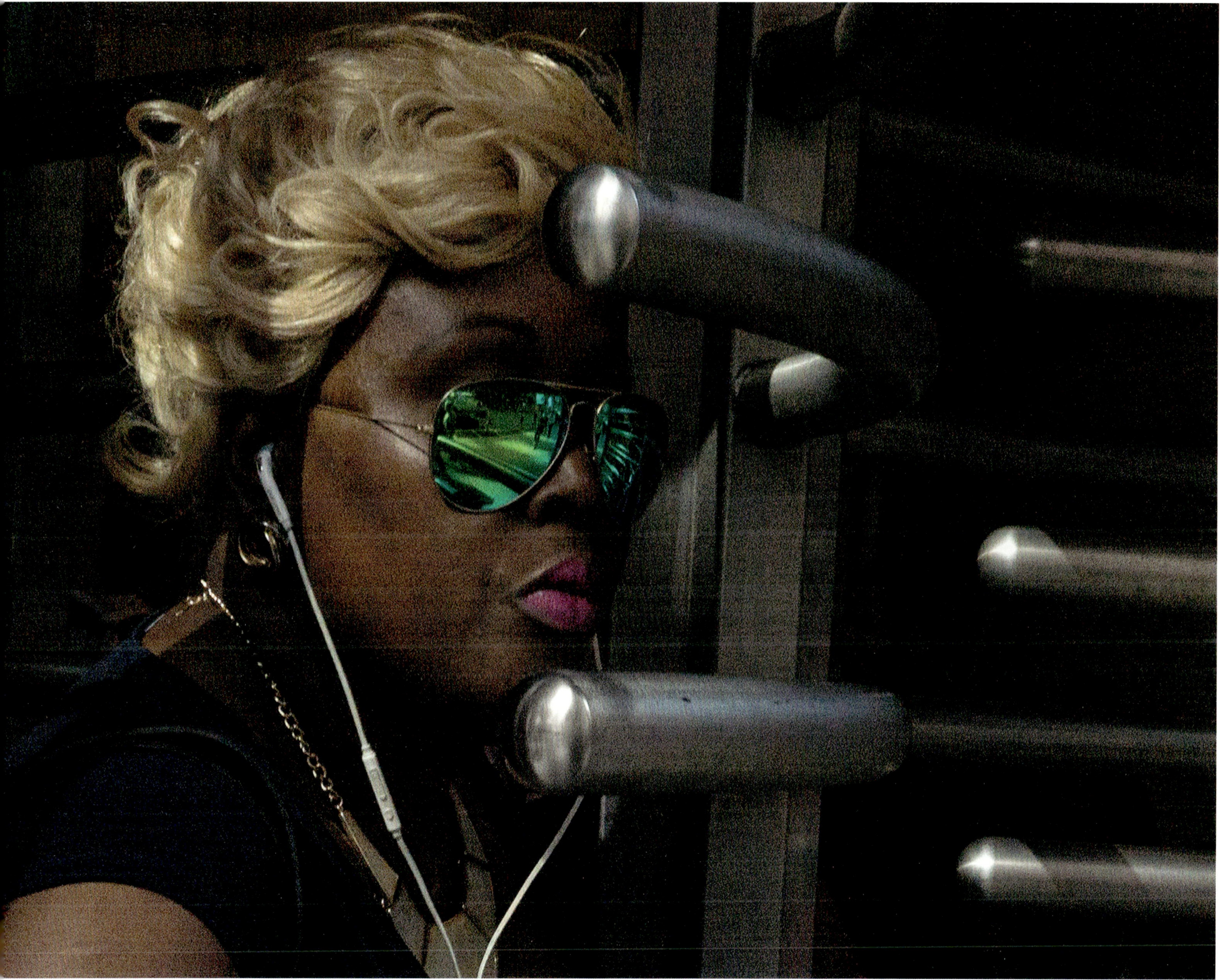

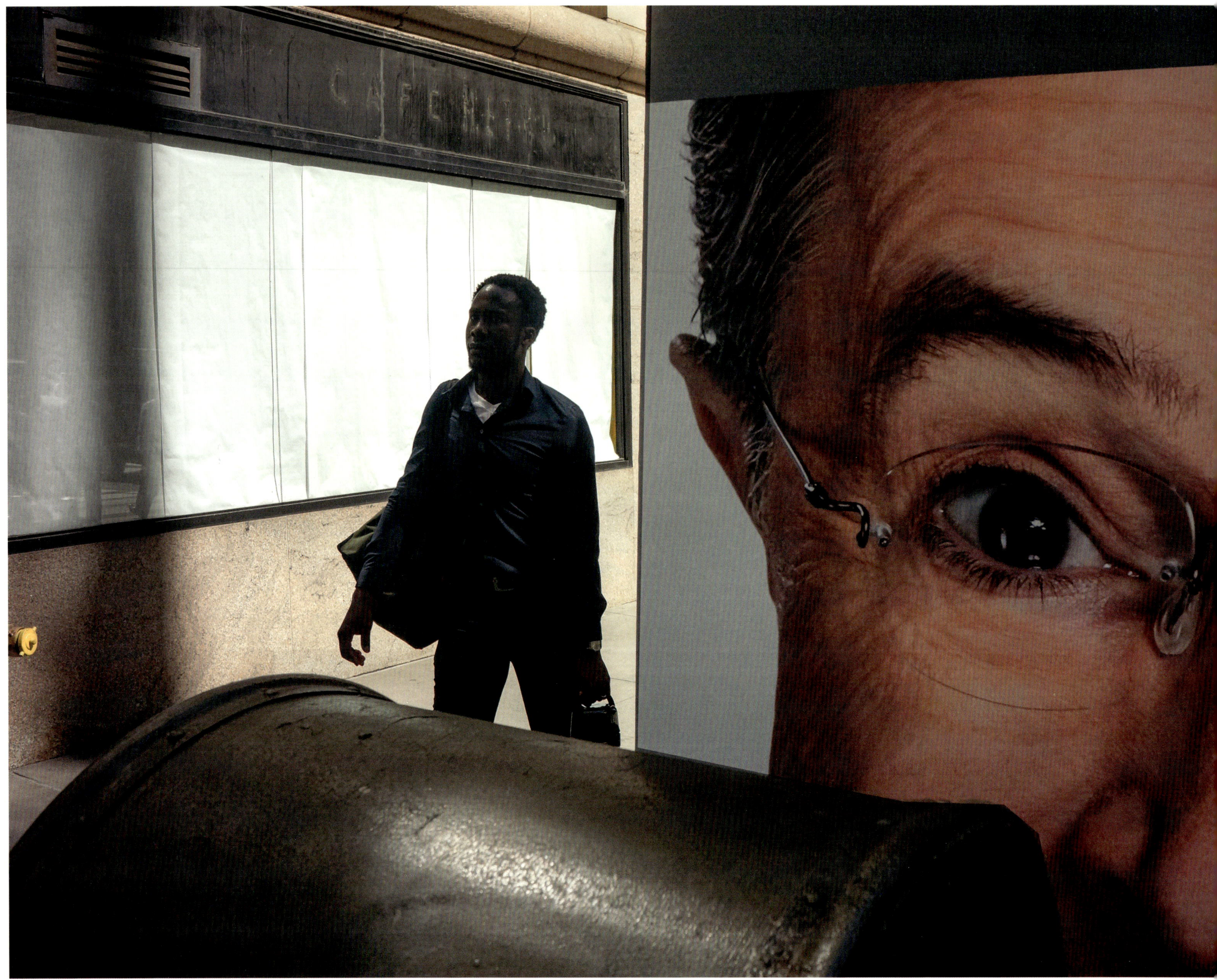

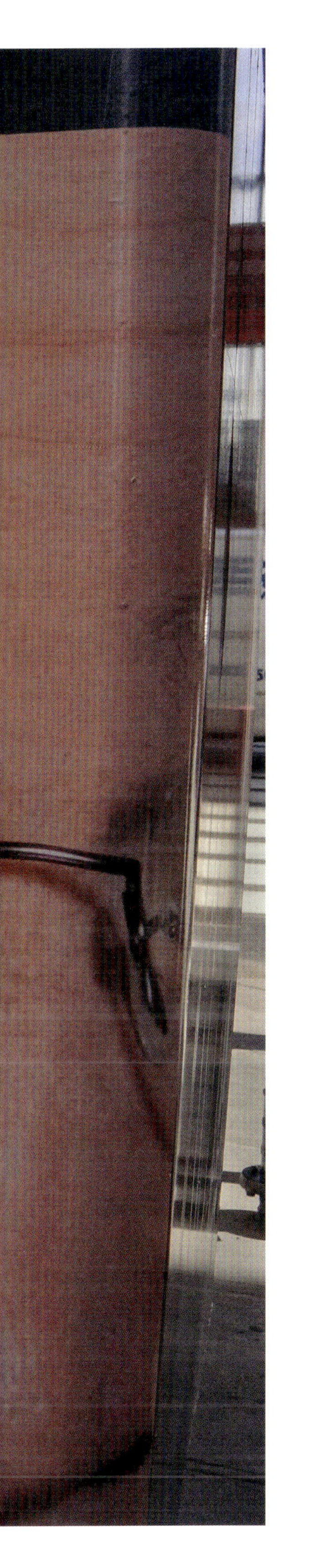

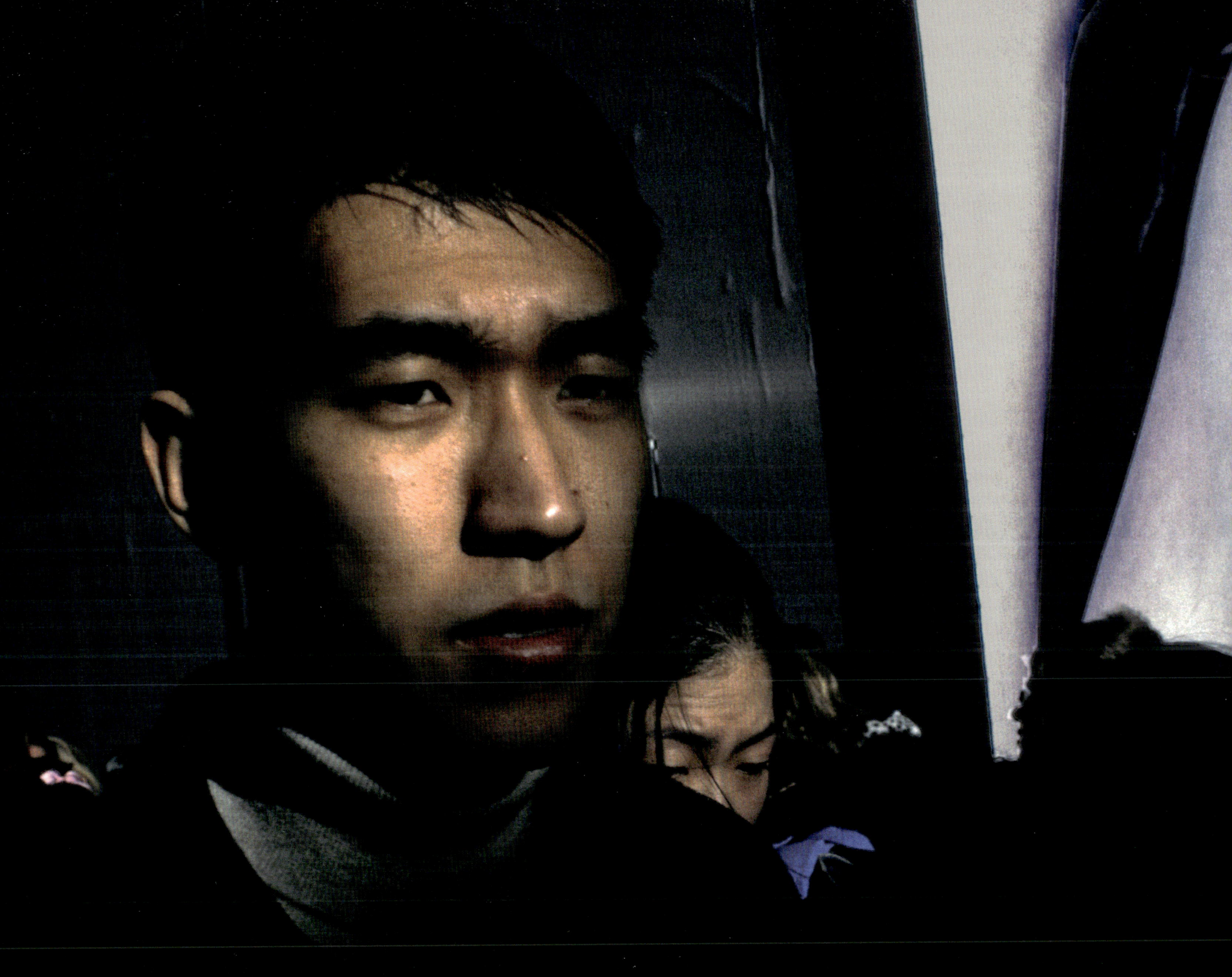

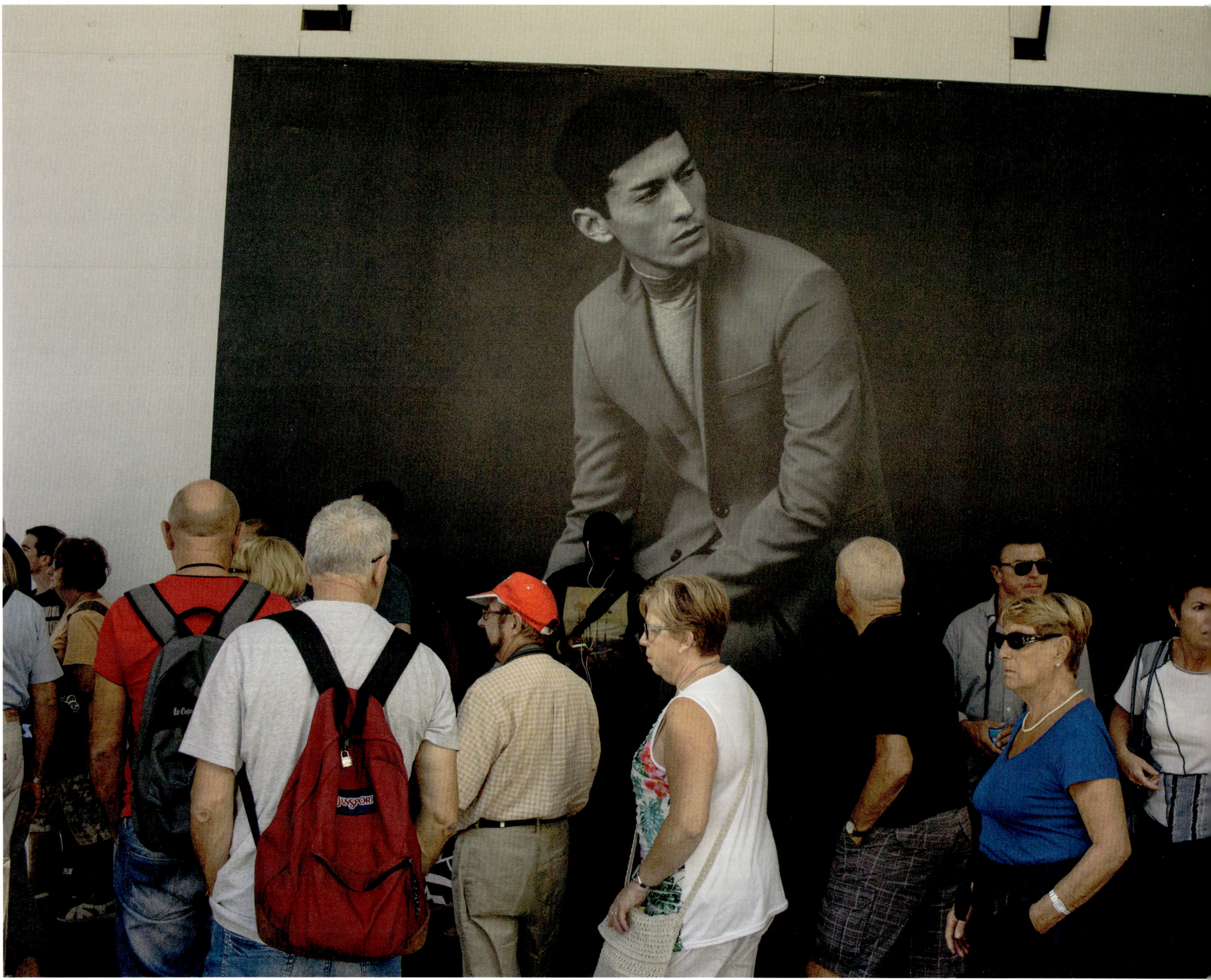

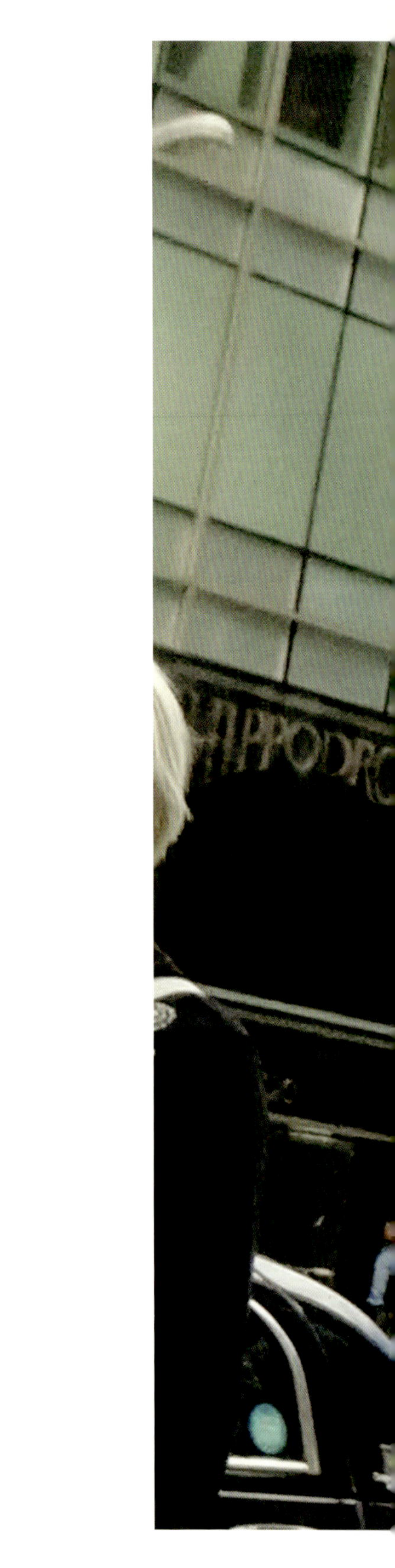
HIPPODR

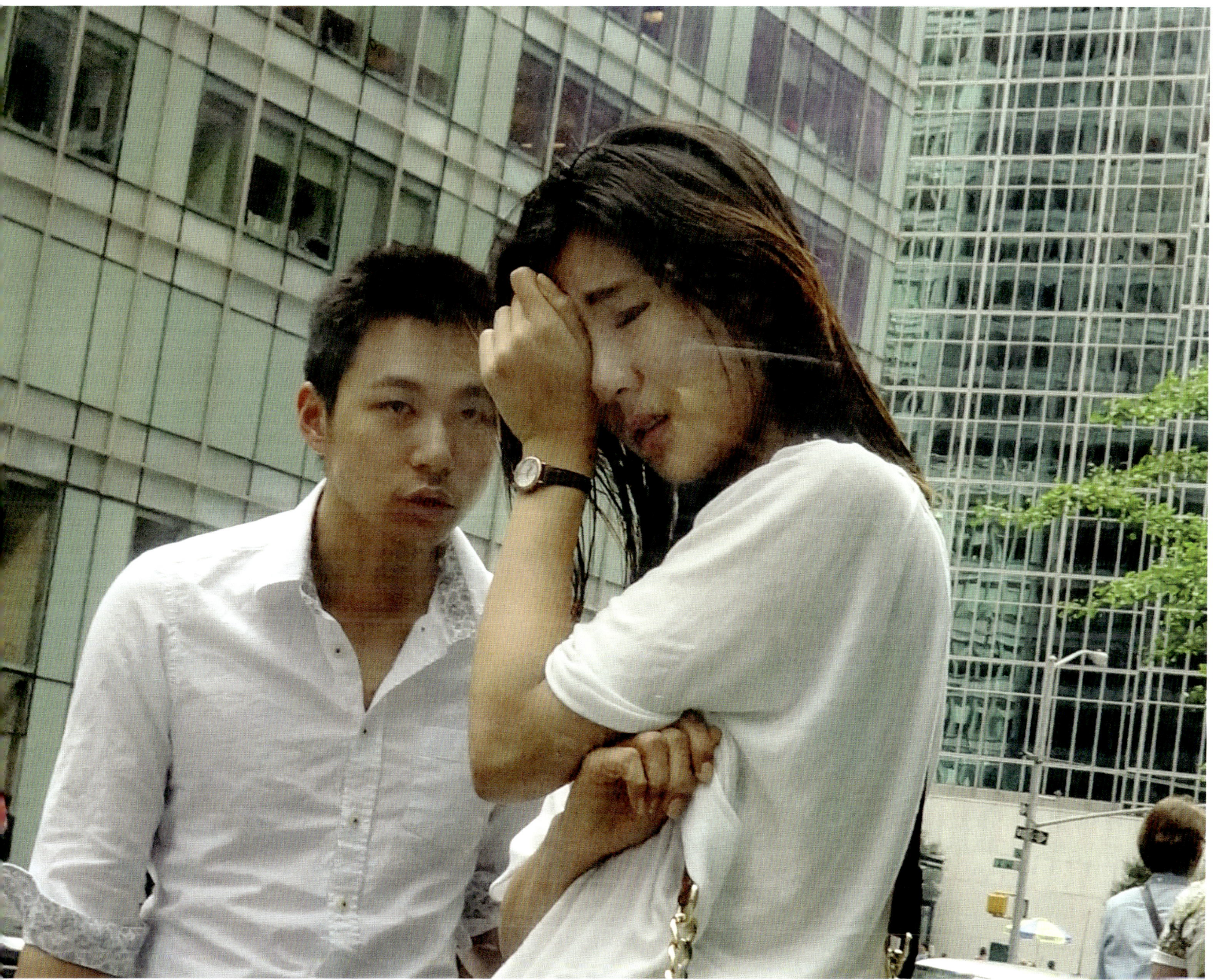

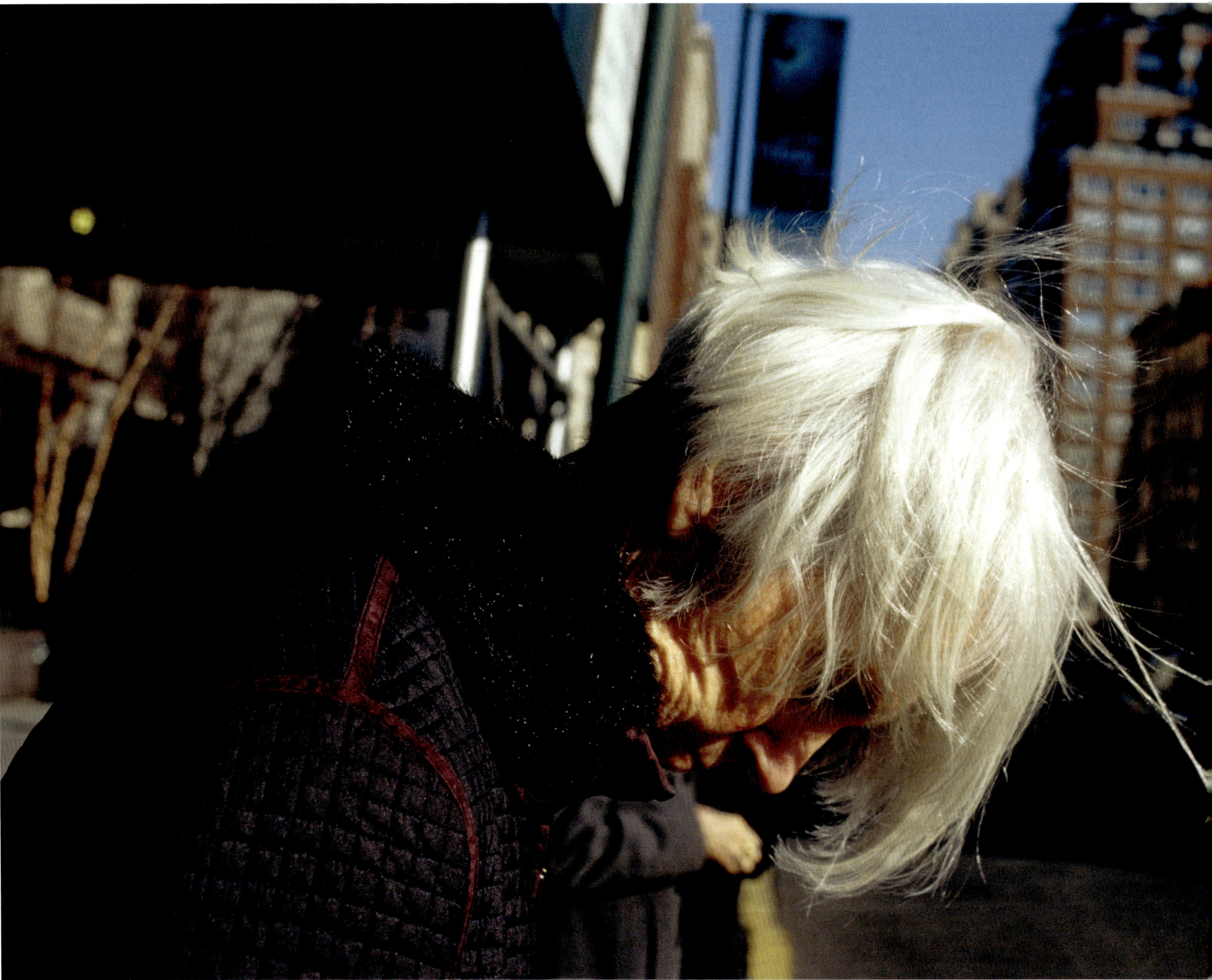

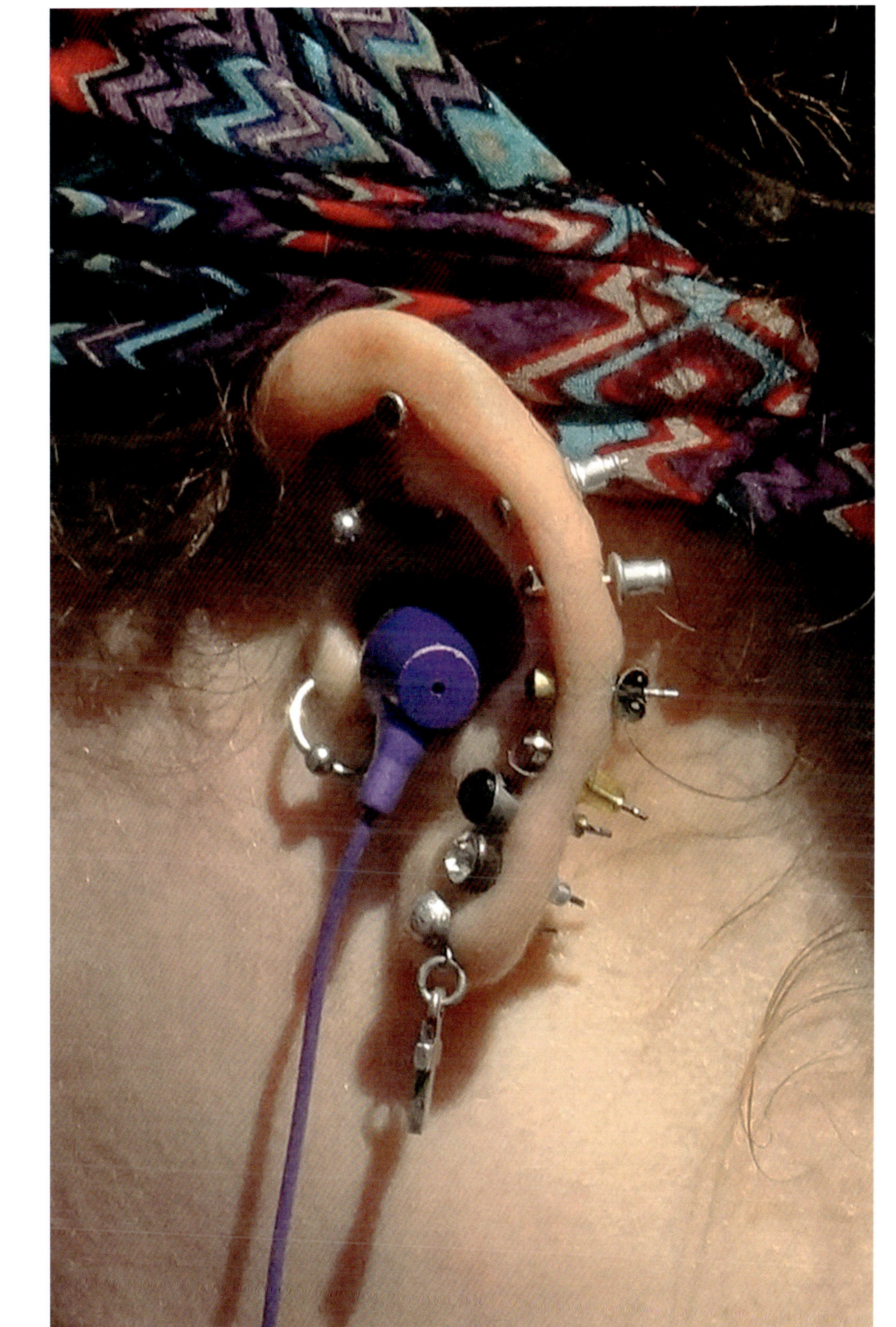

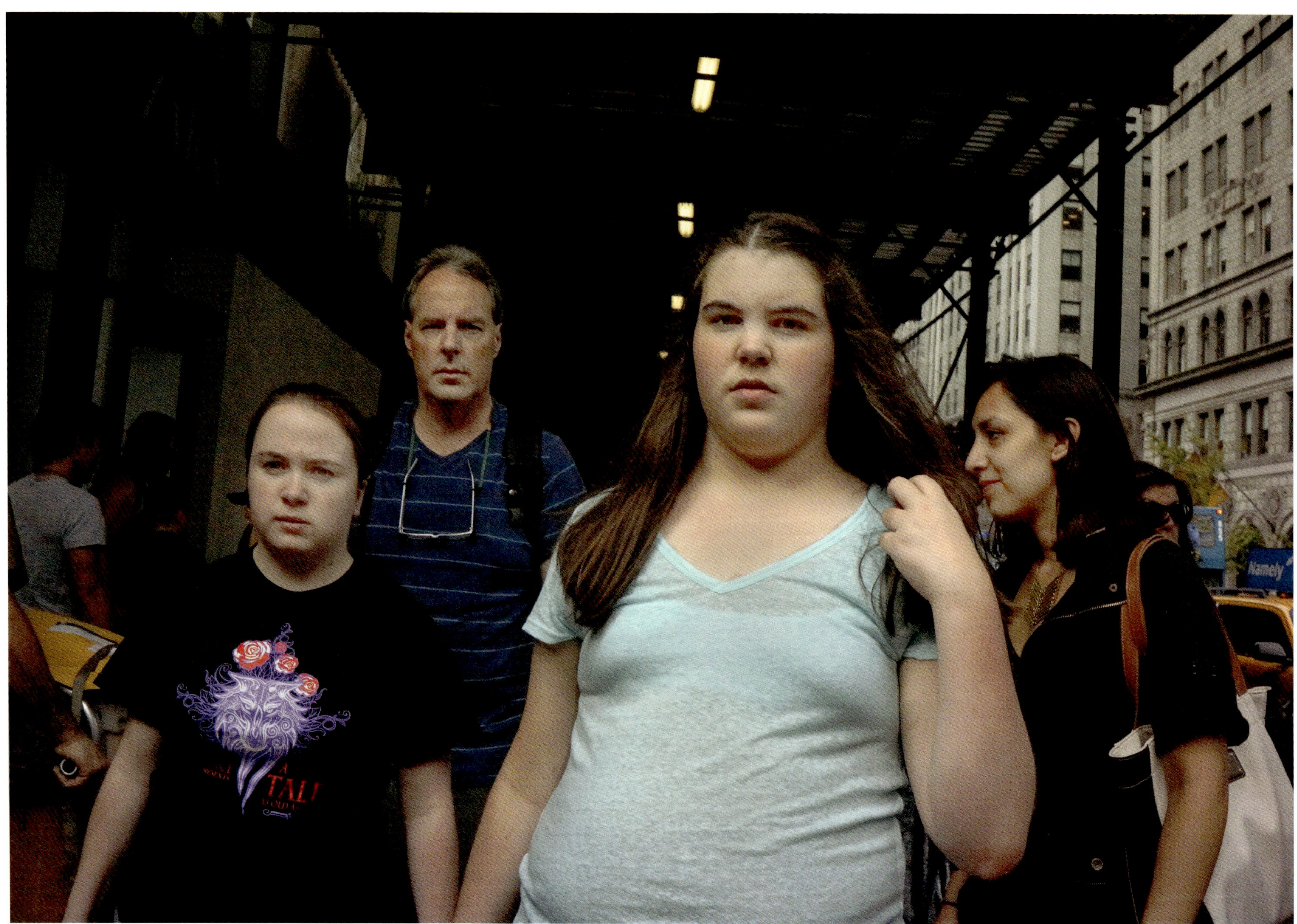

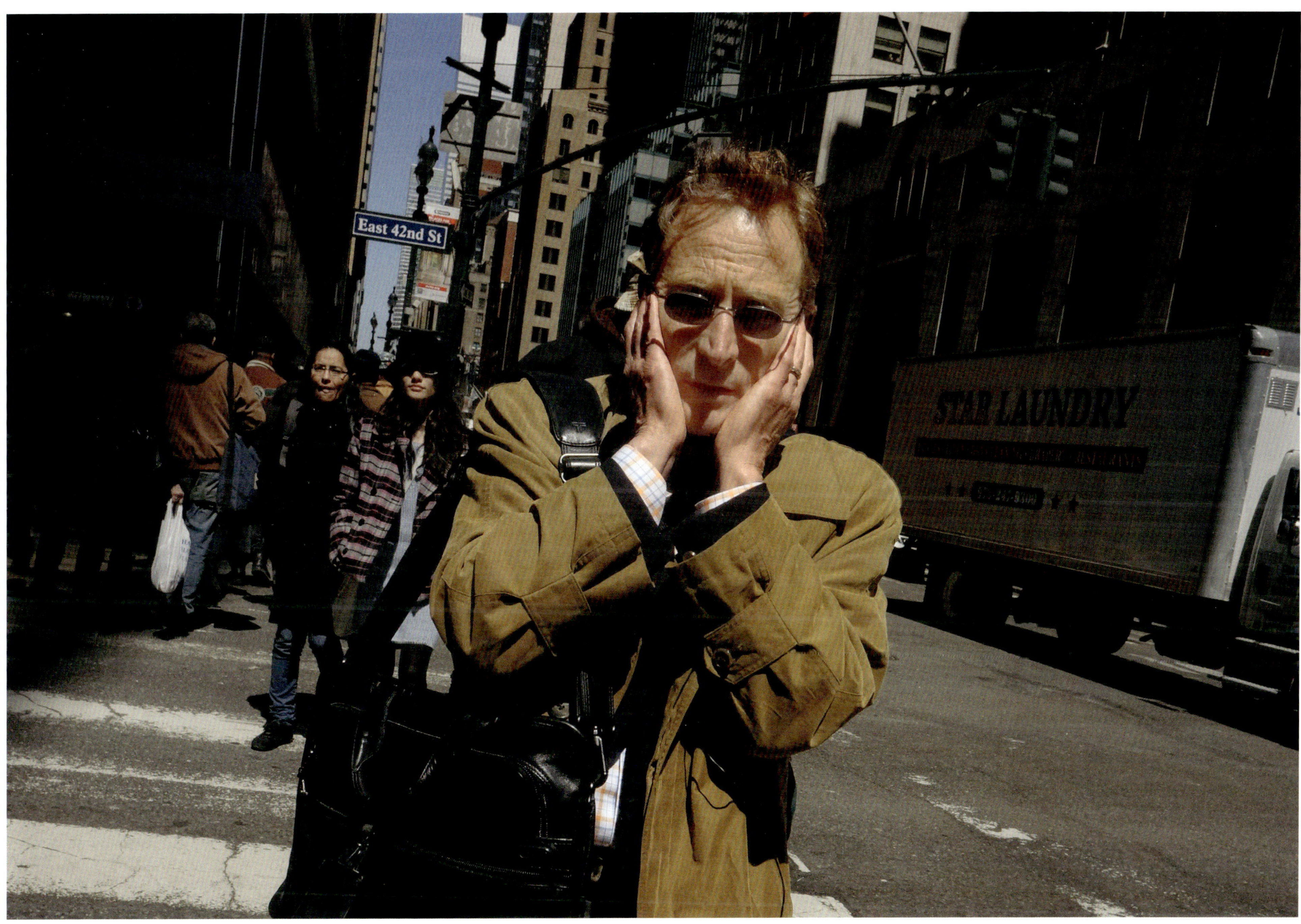

East 42nd St
STAR LAUNDRY

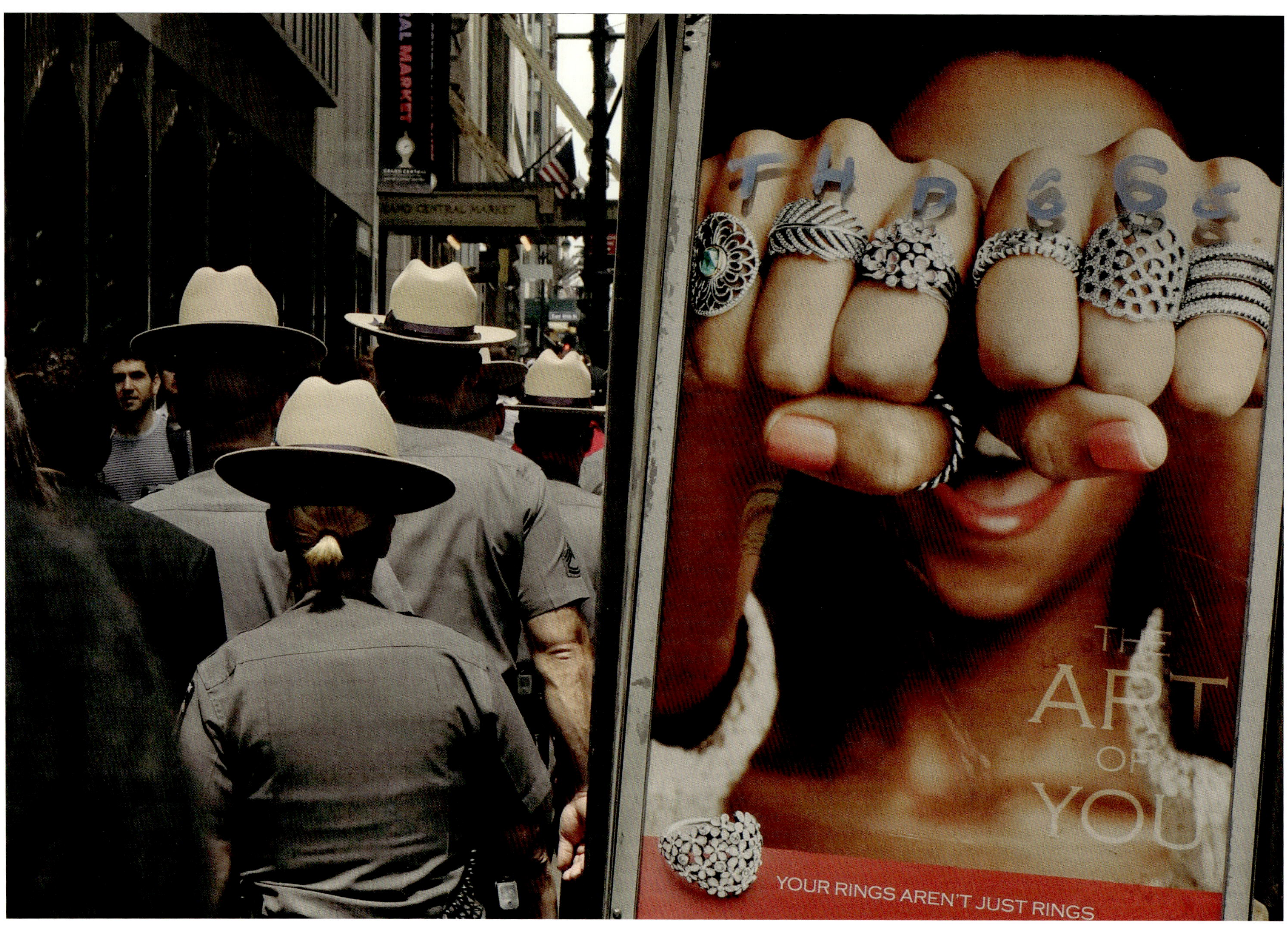
THD665
THE
ART
OF
YOU
YOUR RINGS AREN'T JUST RINGS

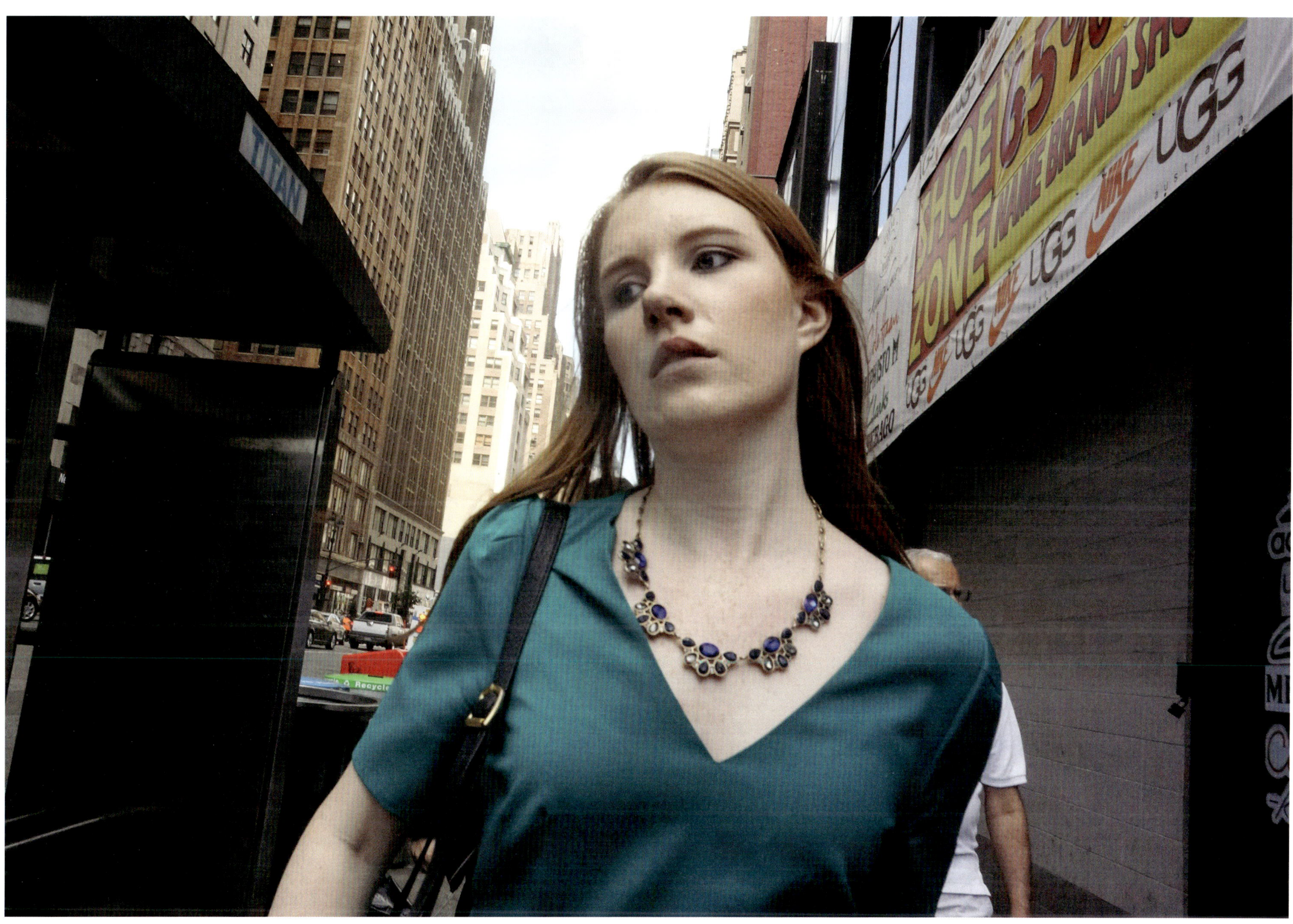

TITAN
SHOE
ZONE NAME BRAND SHO
UGG
NIKE
UGG
australia

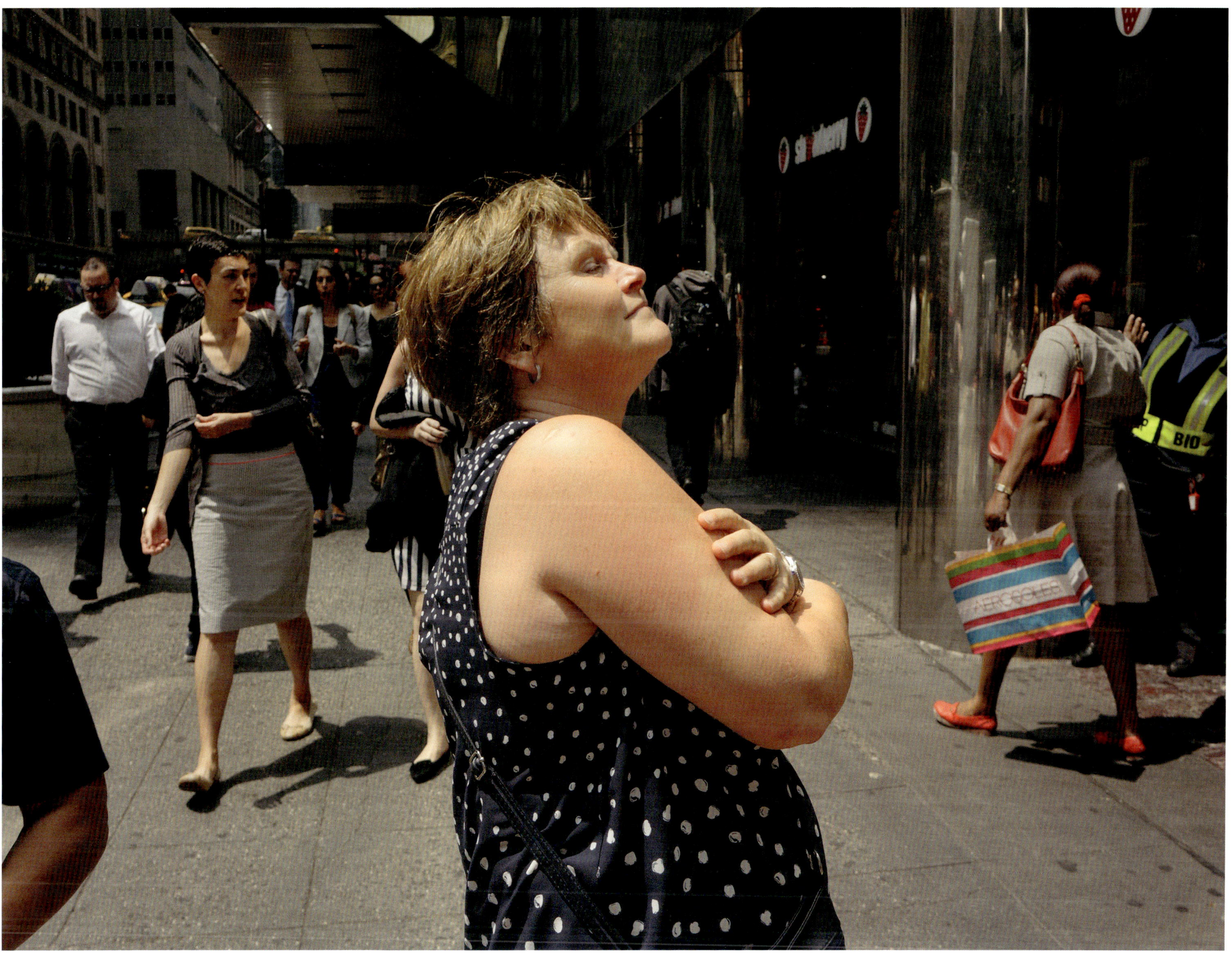

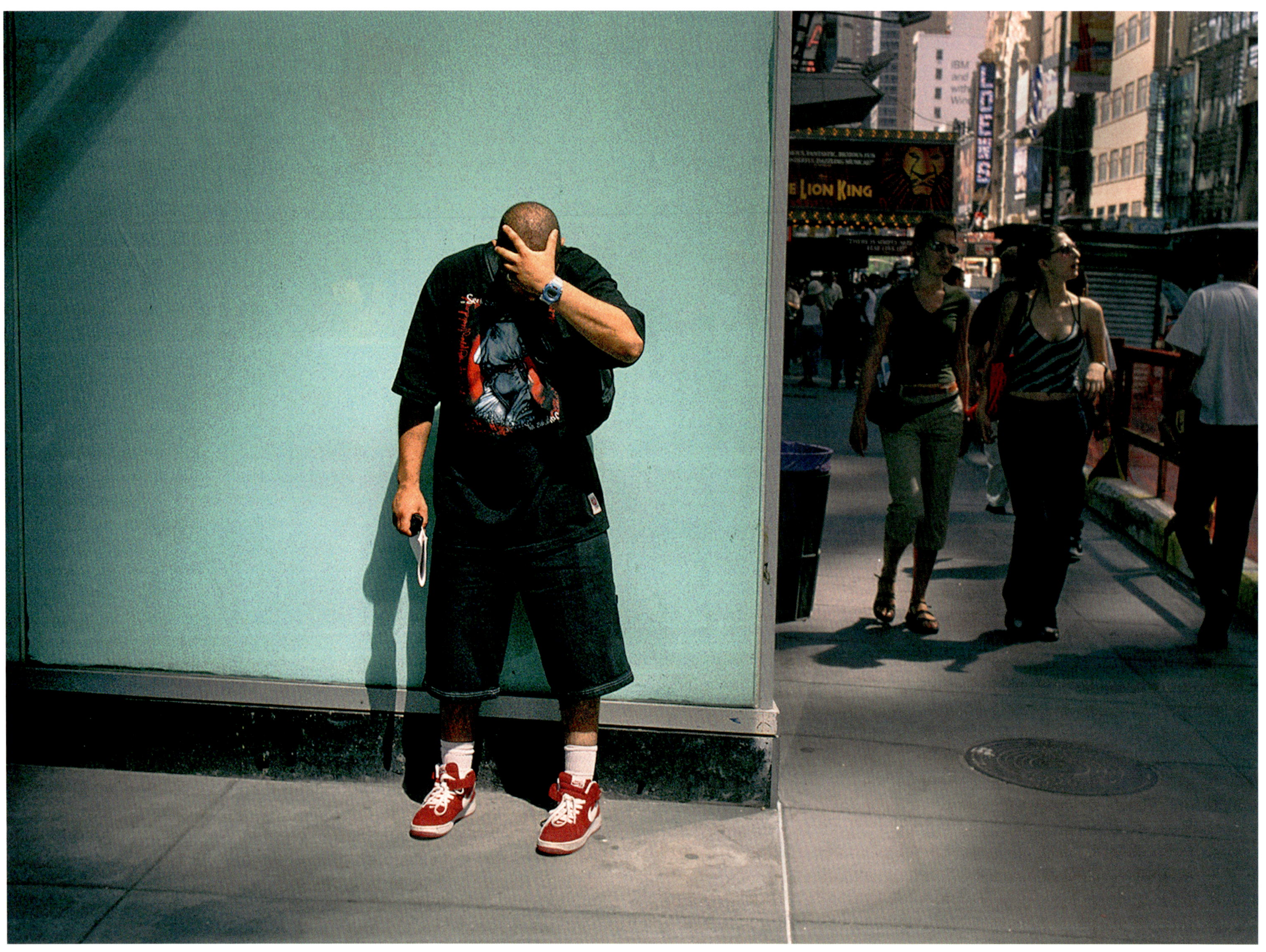

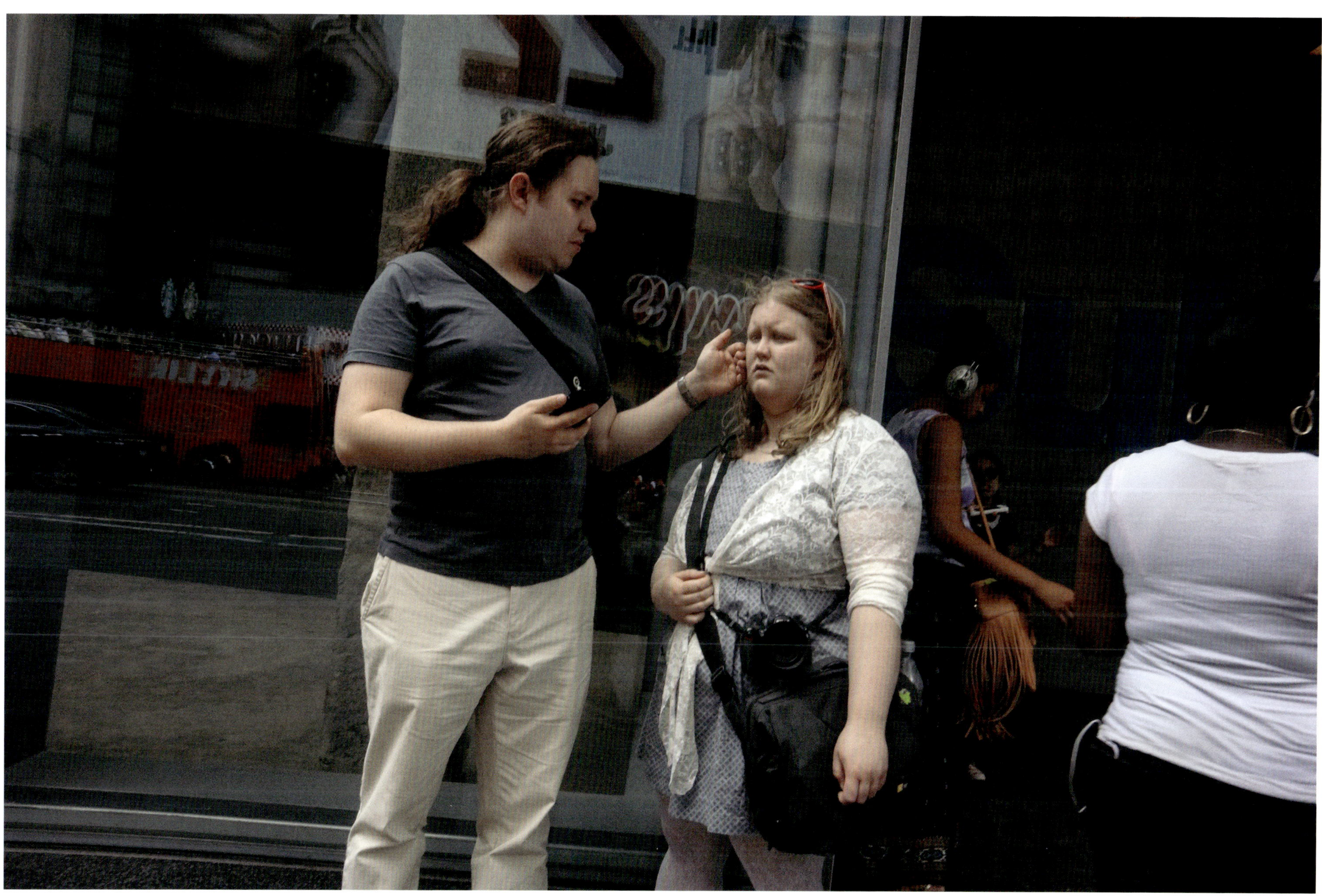

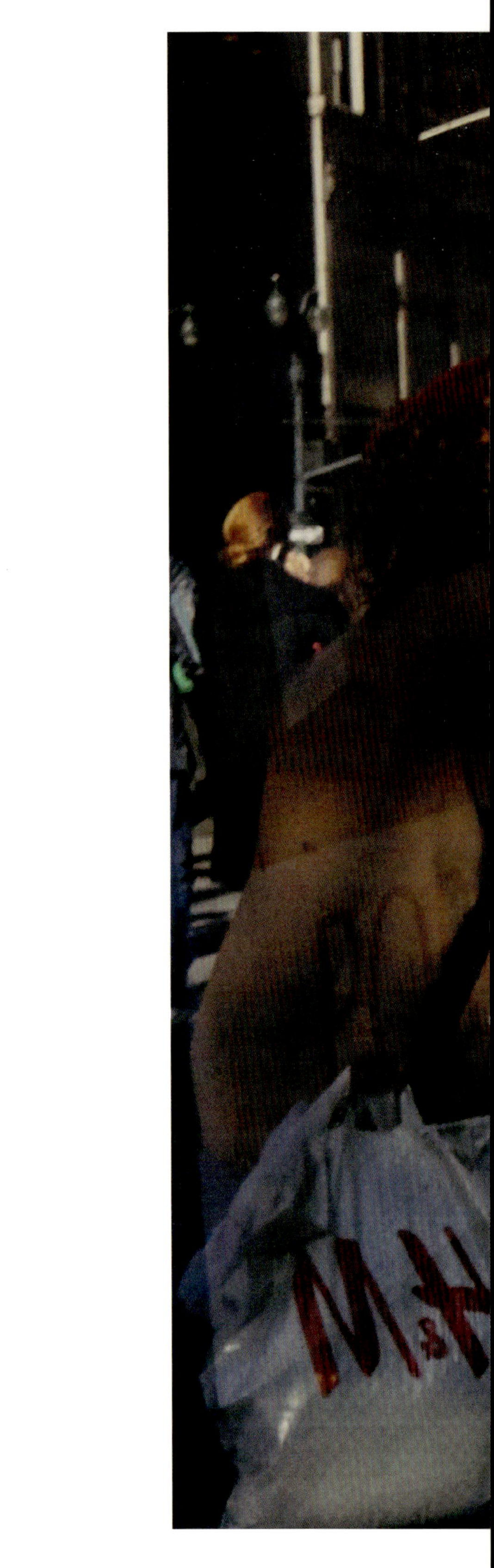

M&

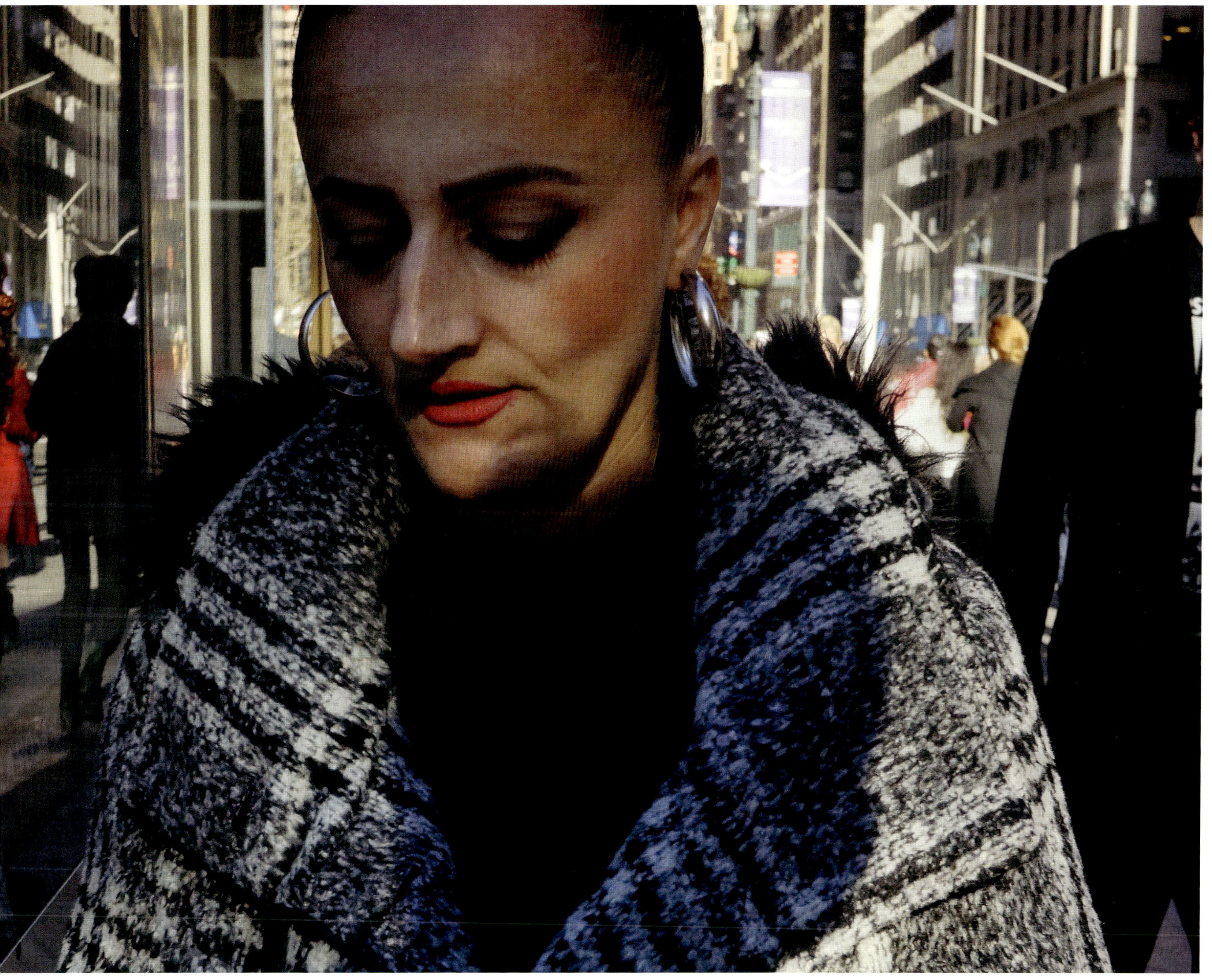

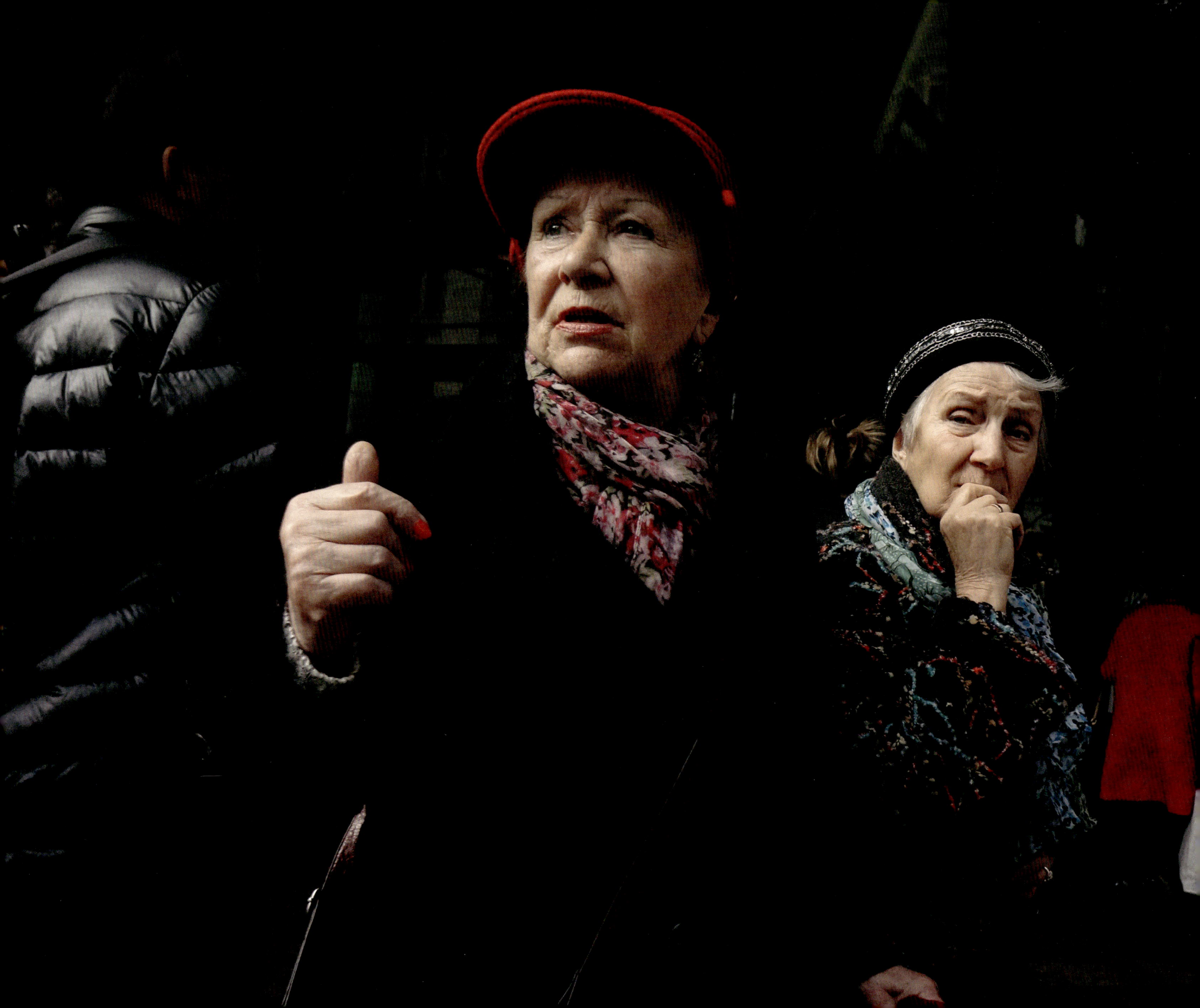

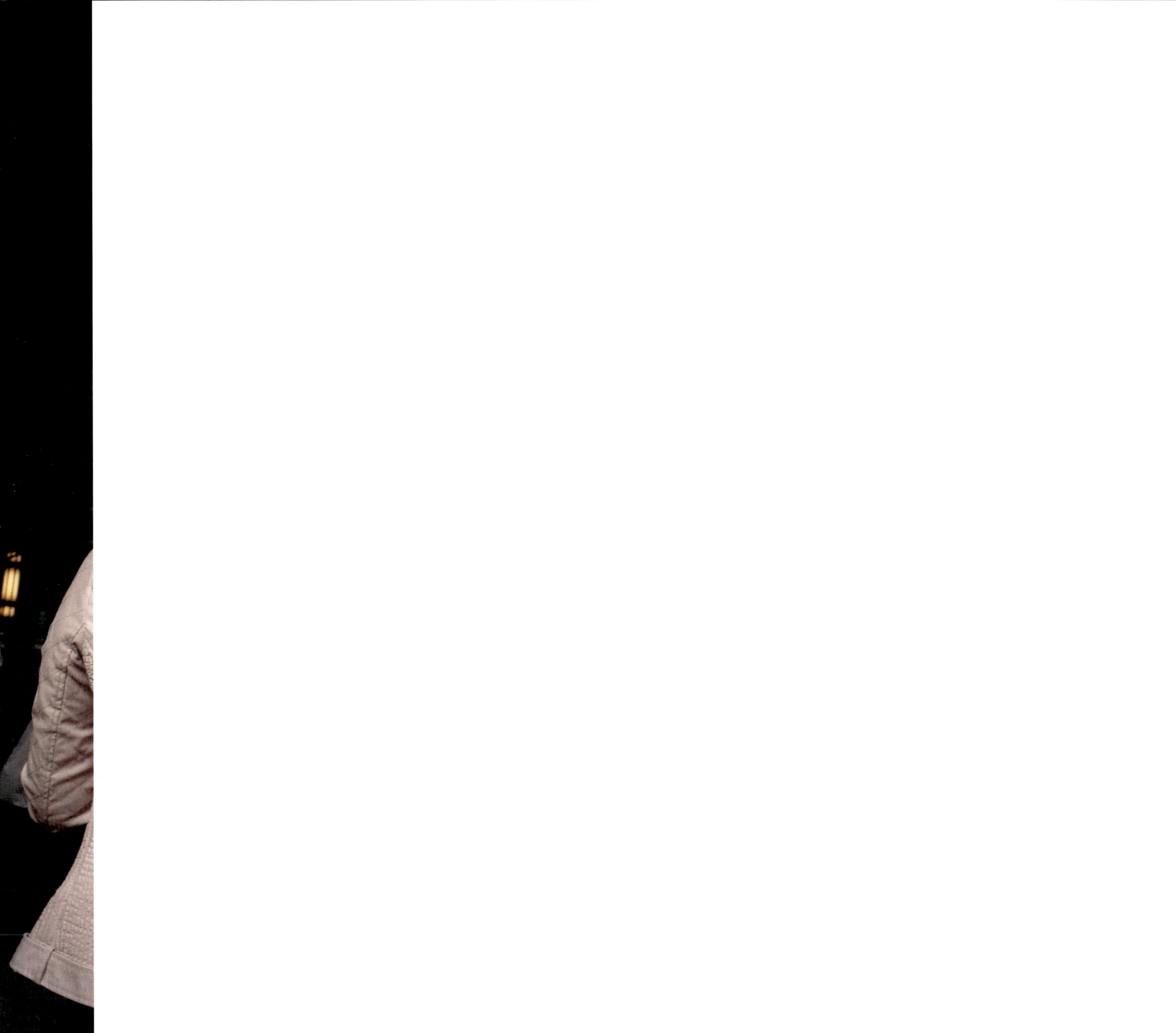

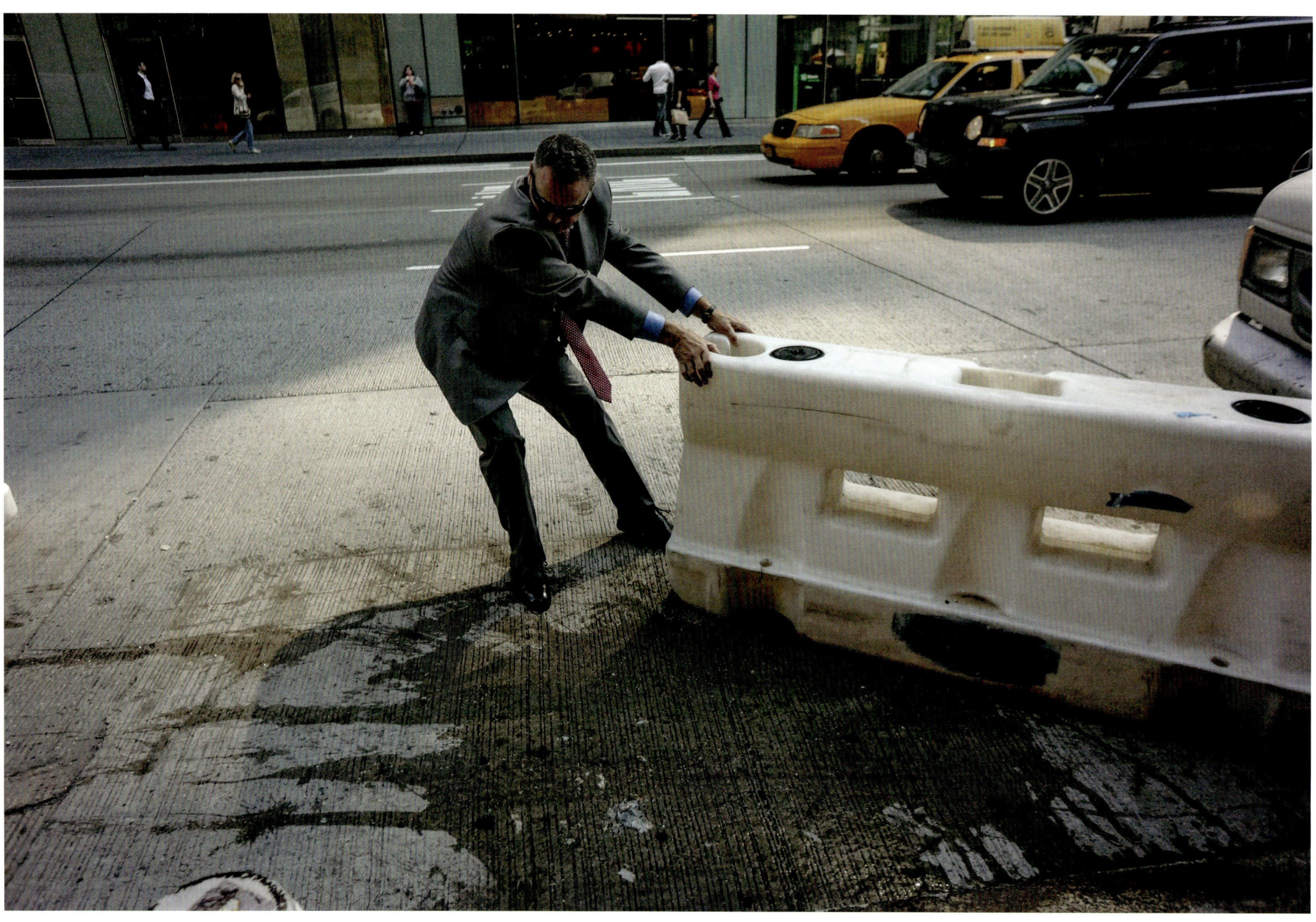

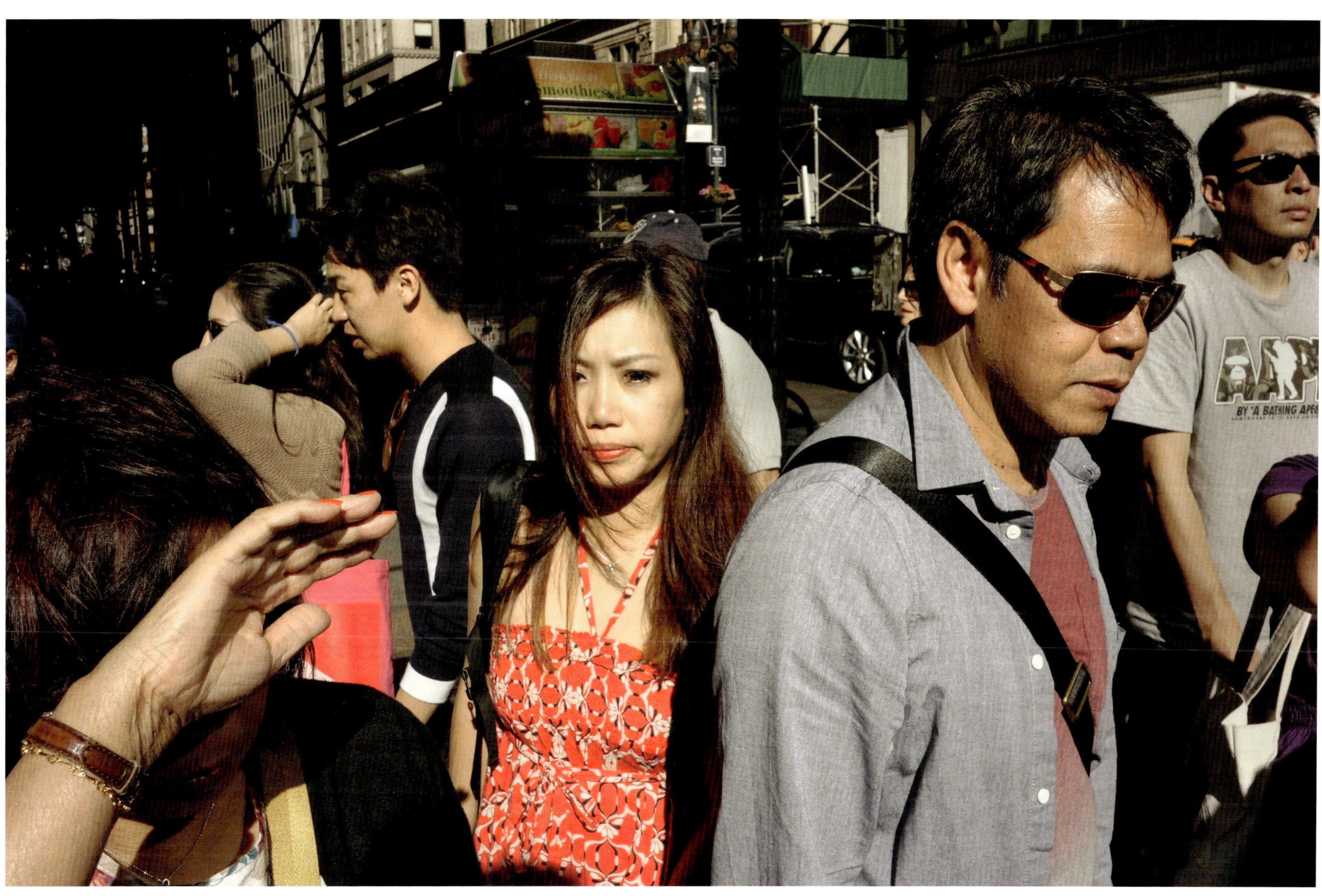

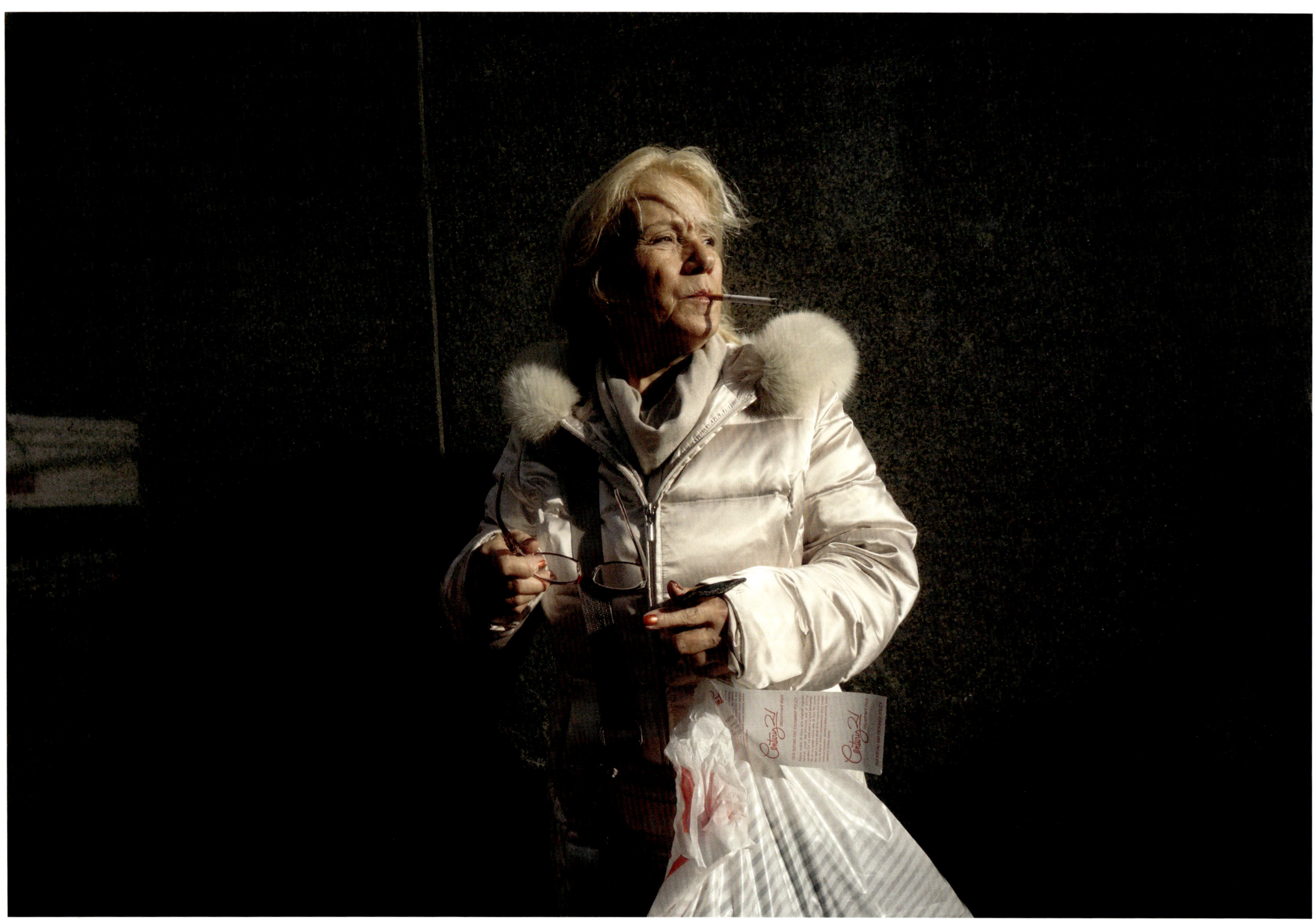

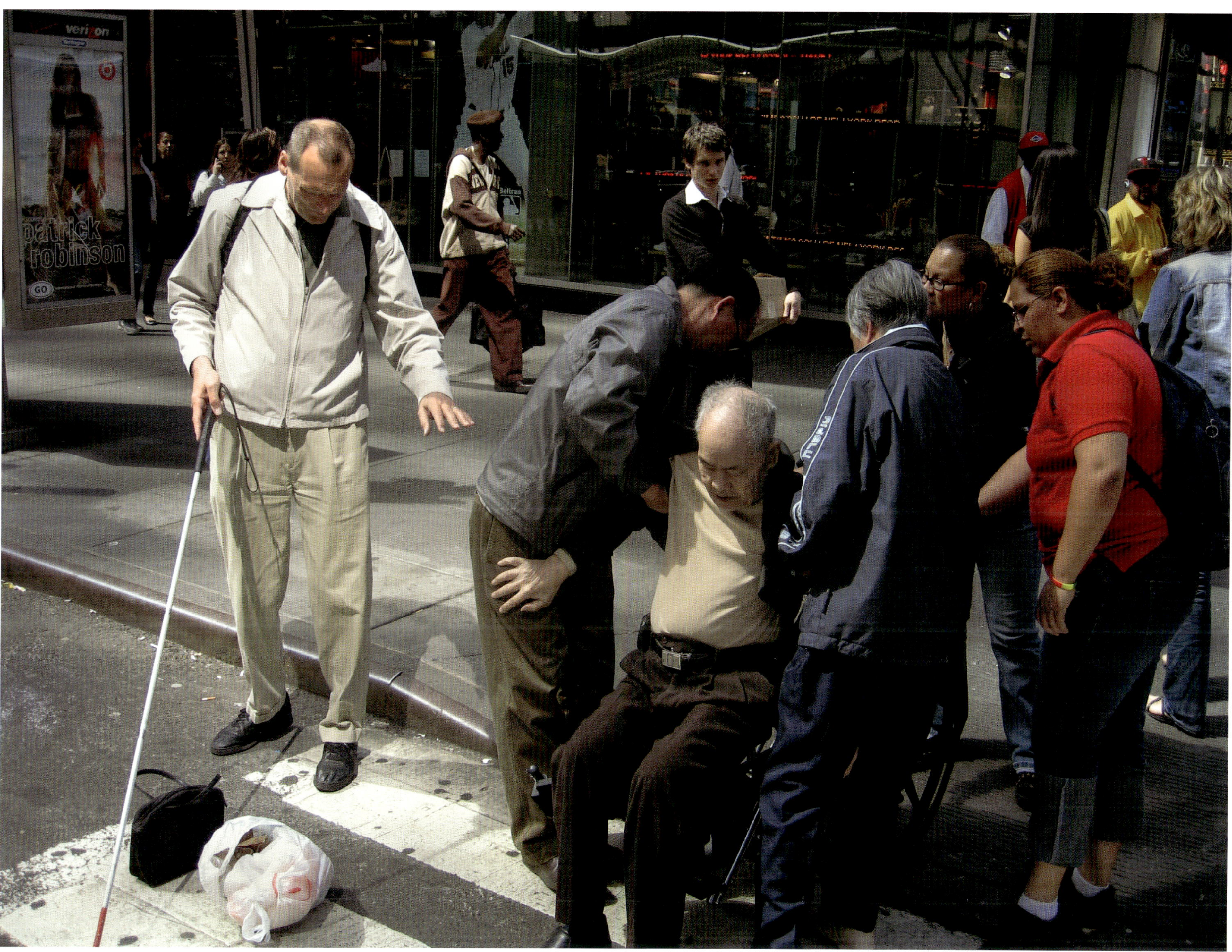

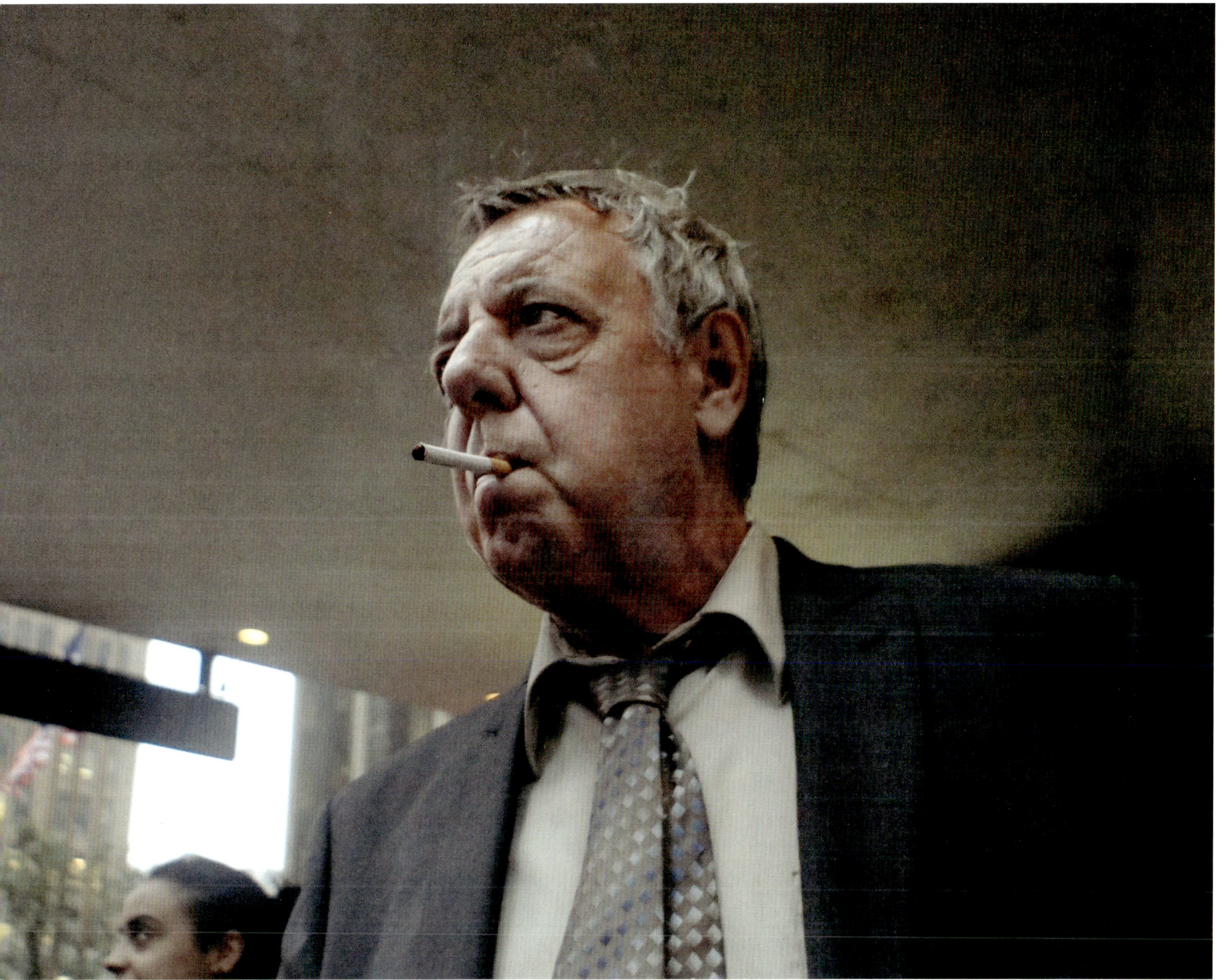

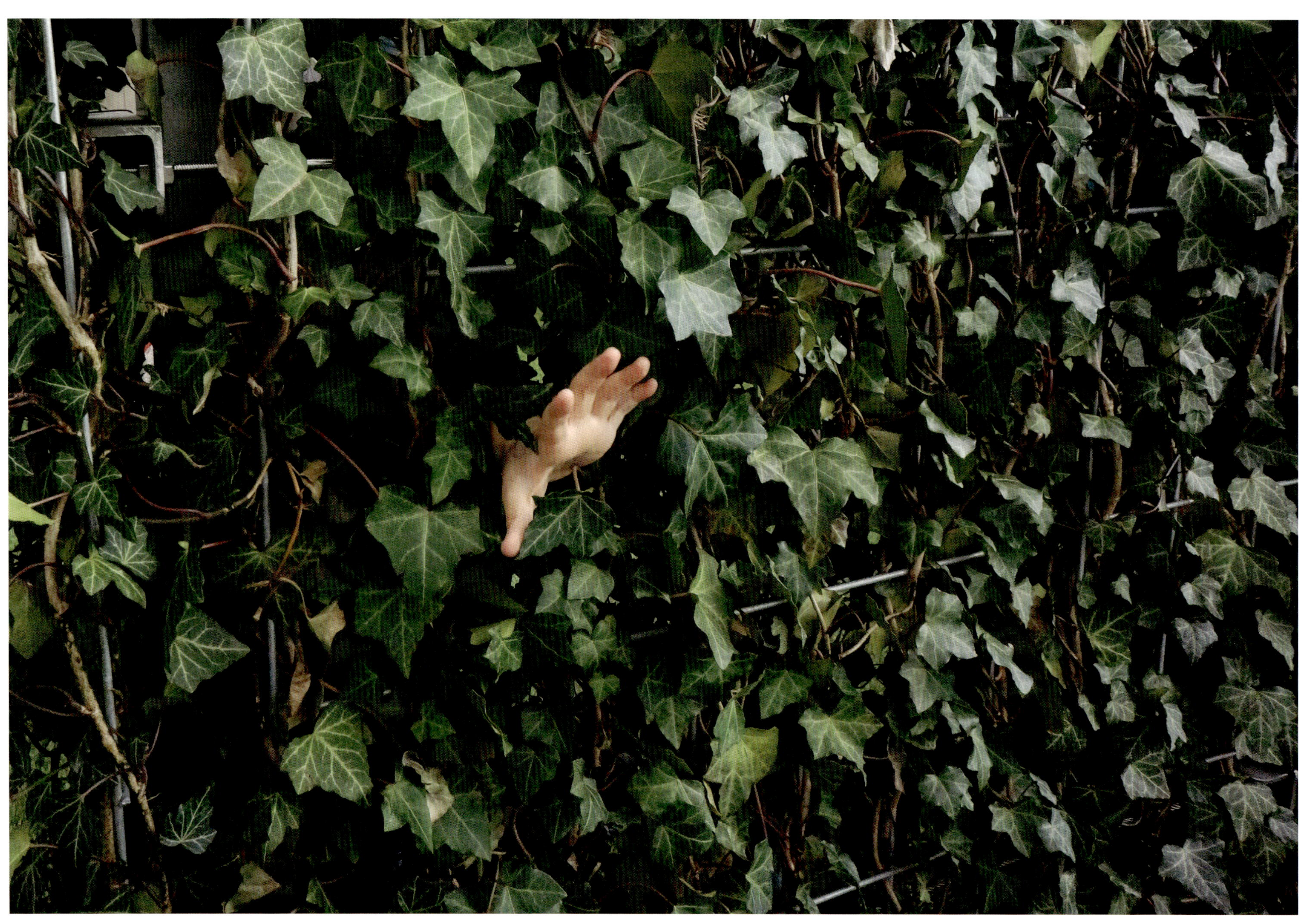

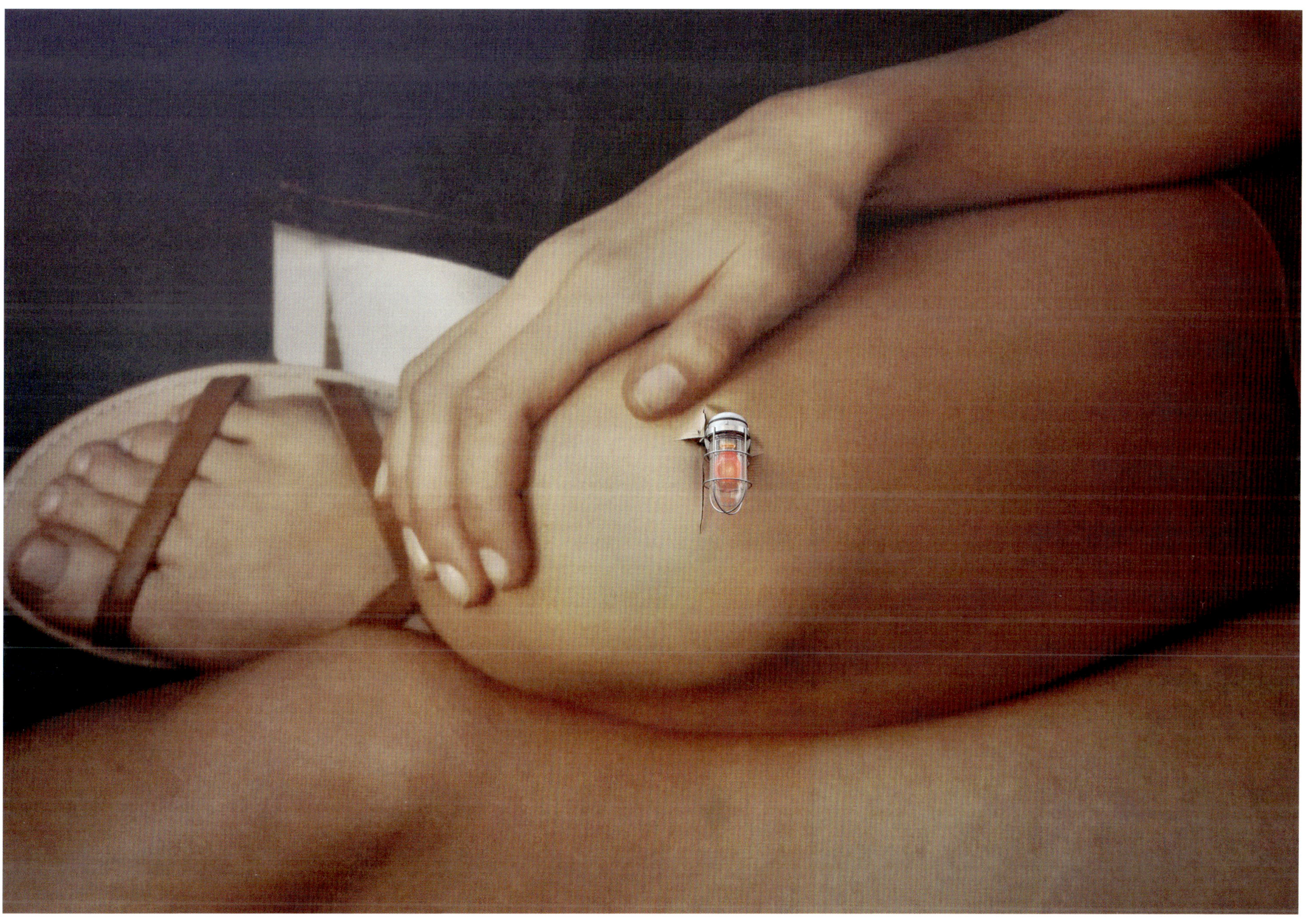

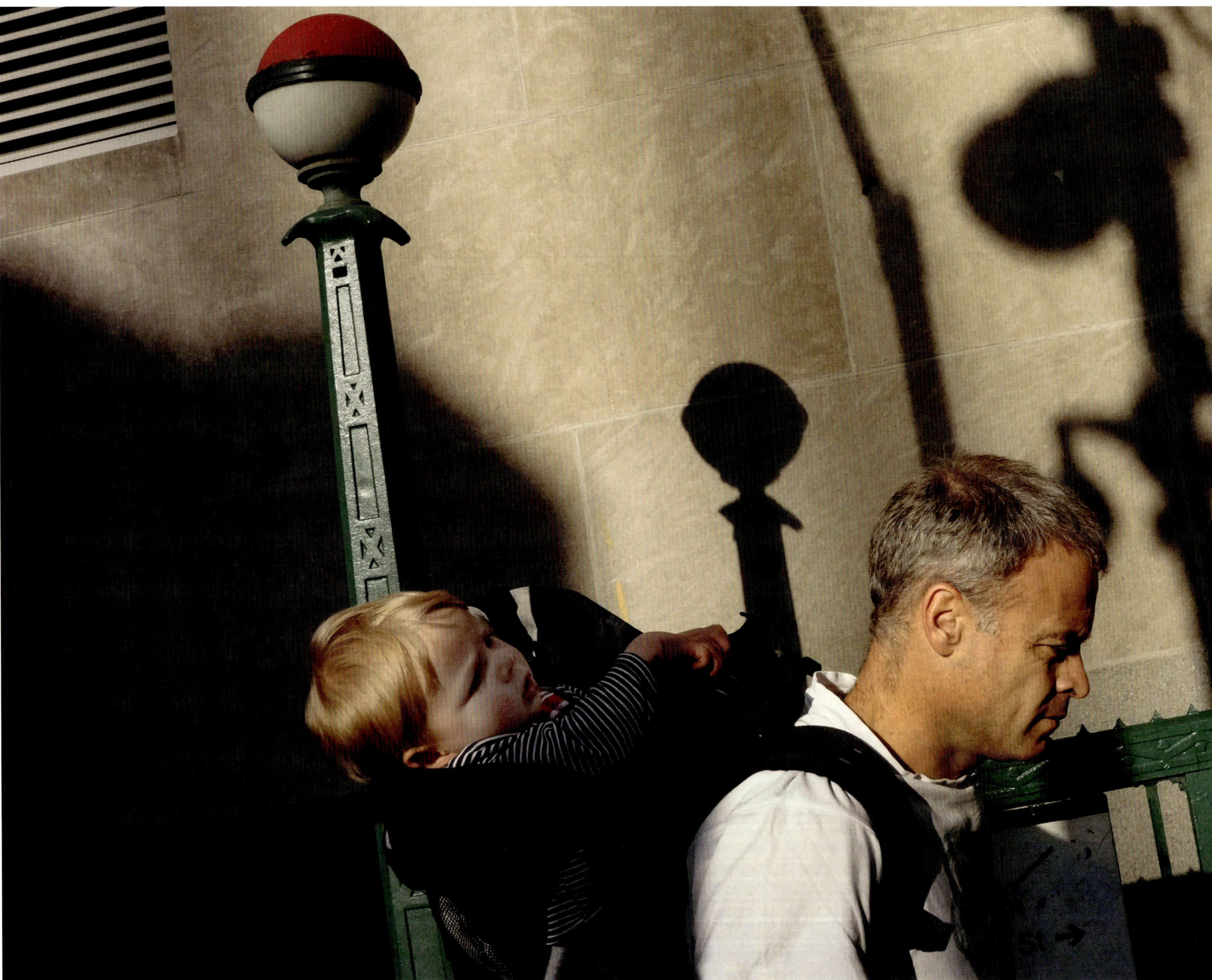

Subw

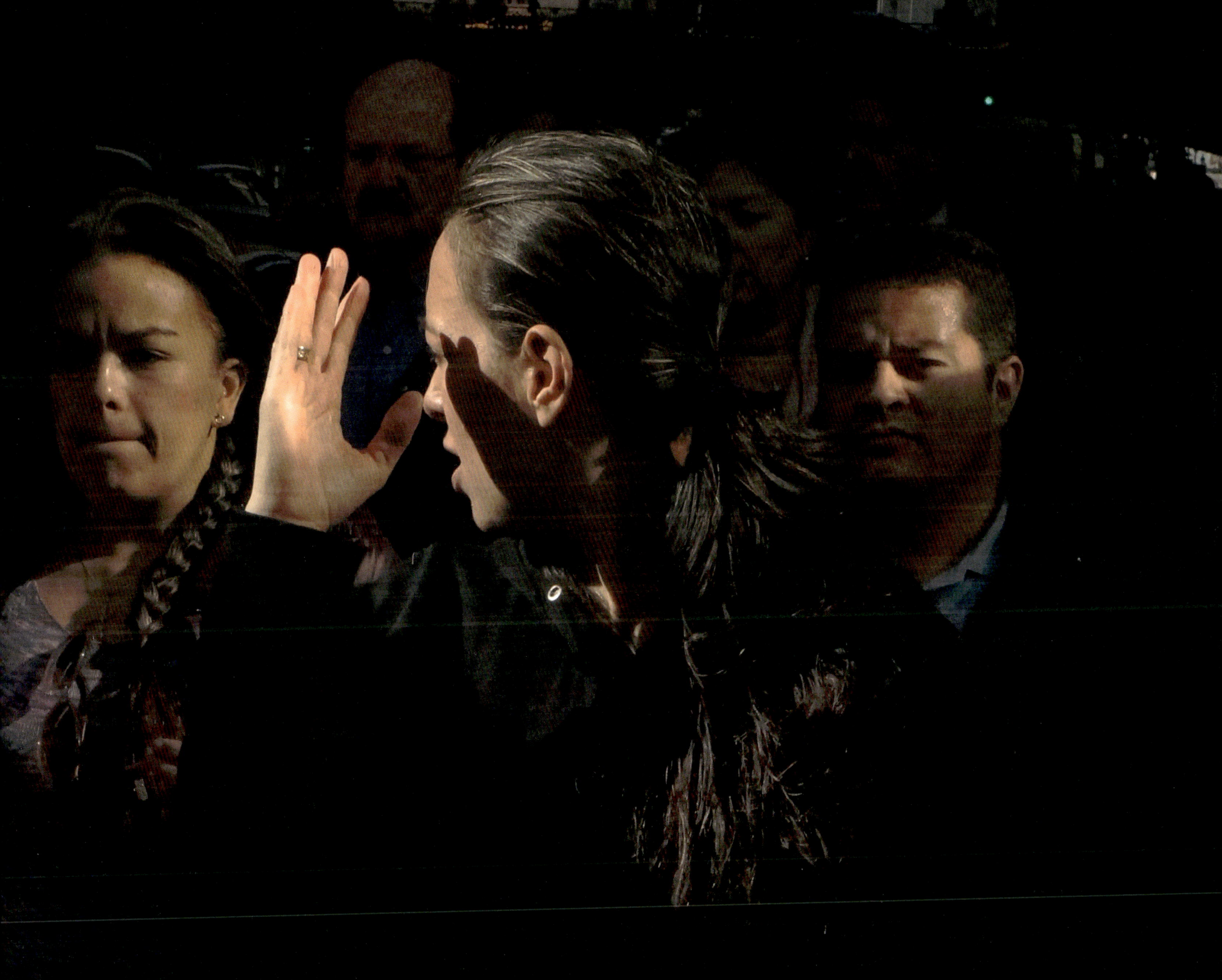

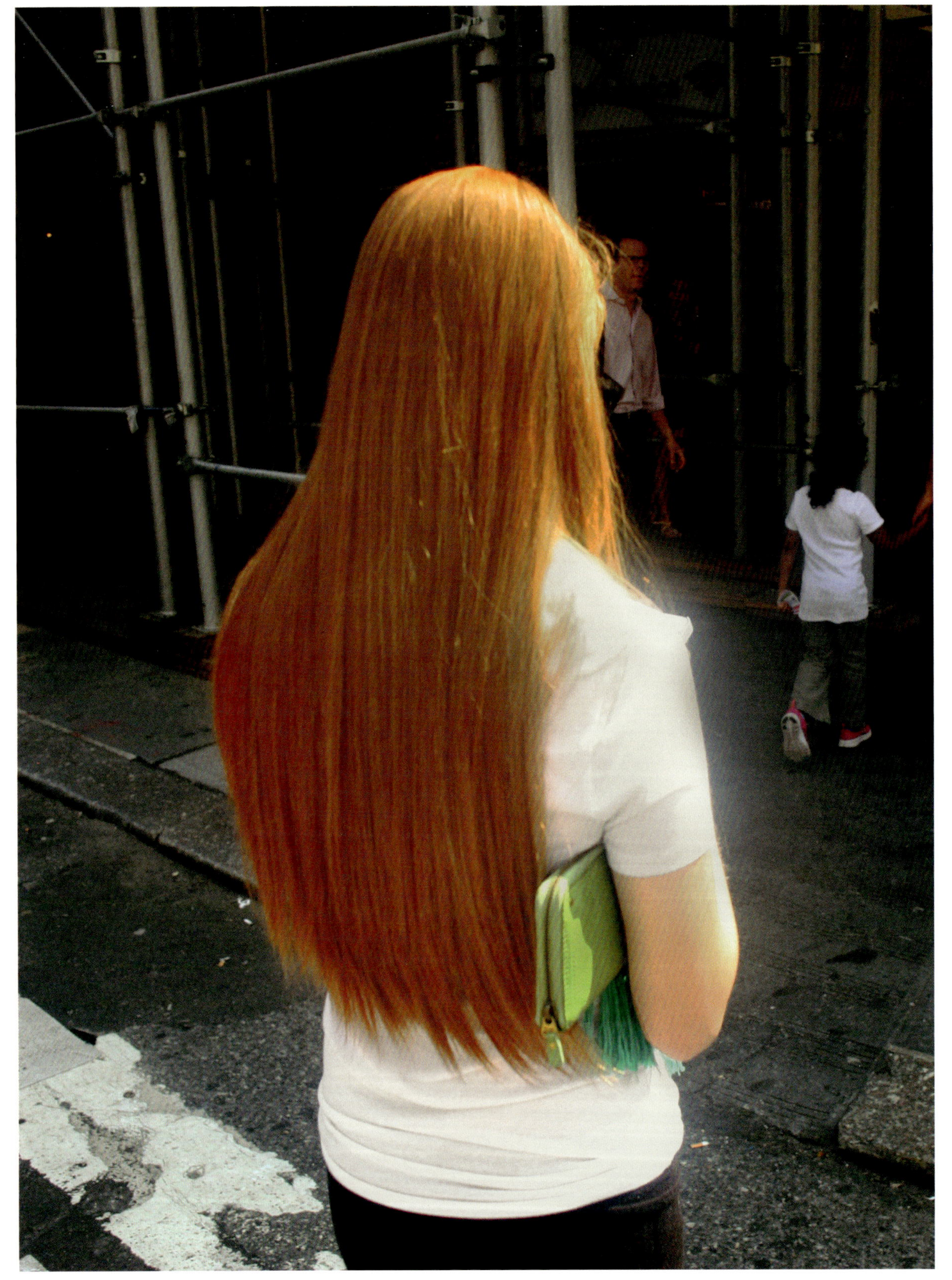

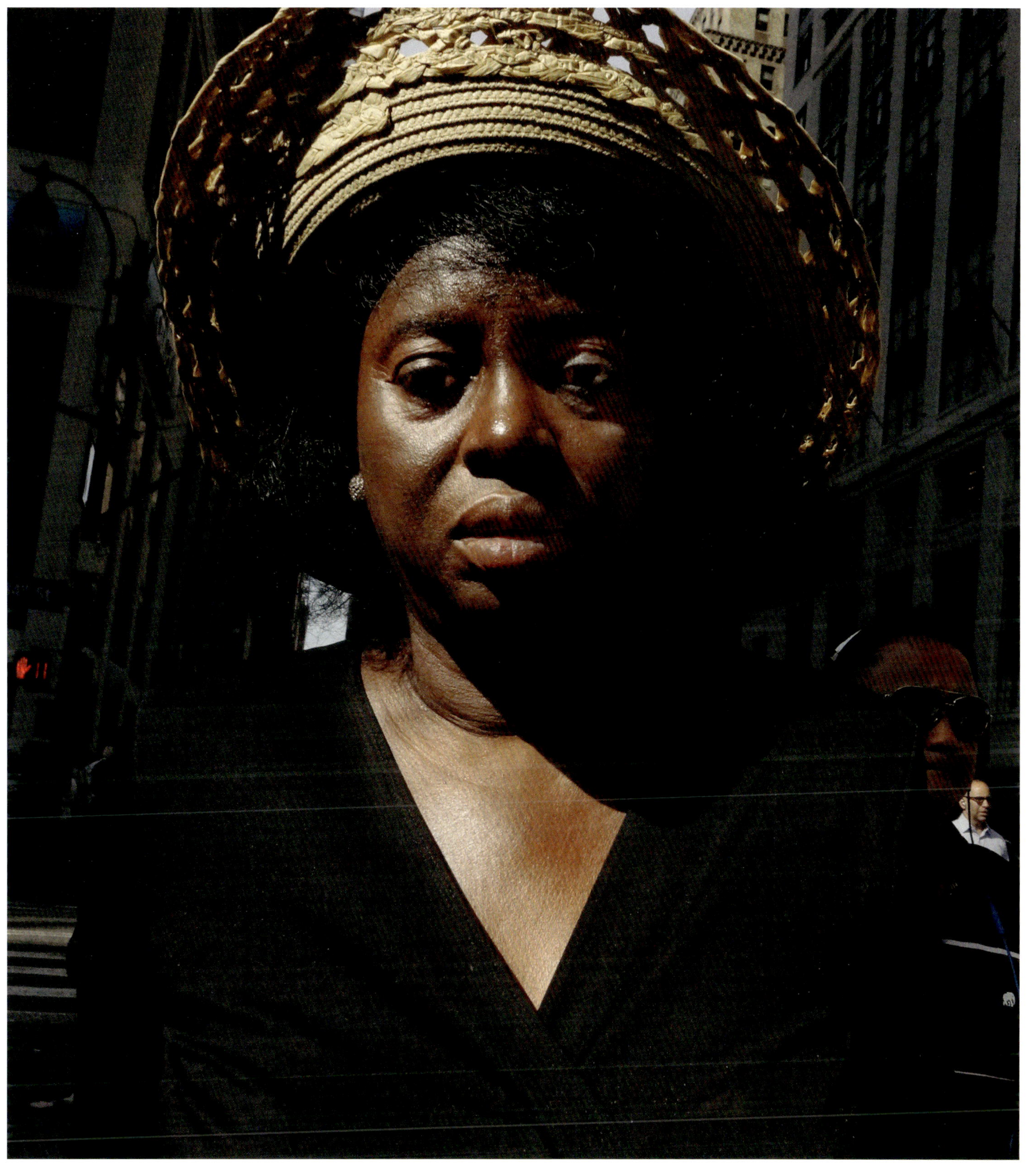

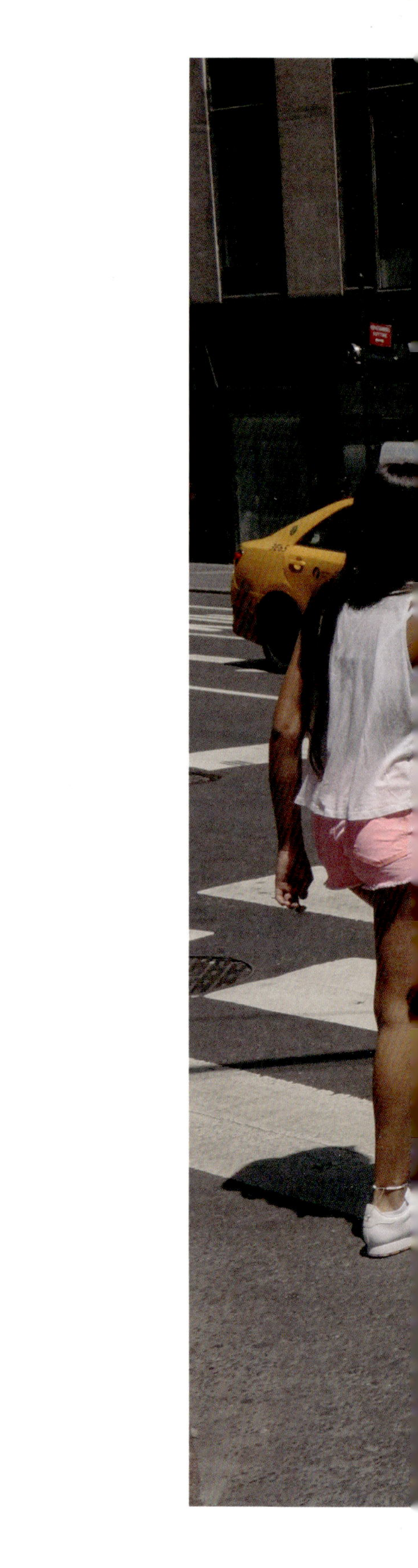

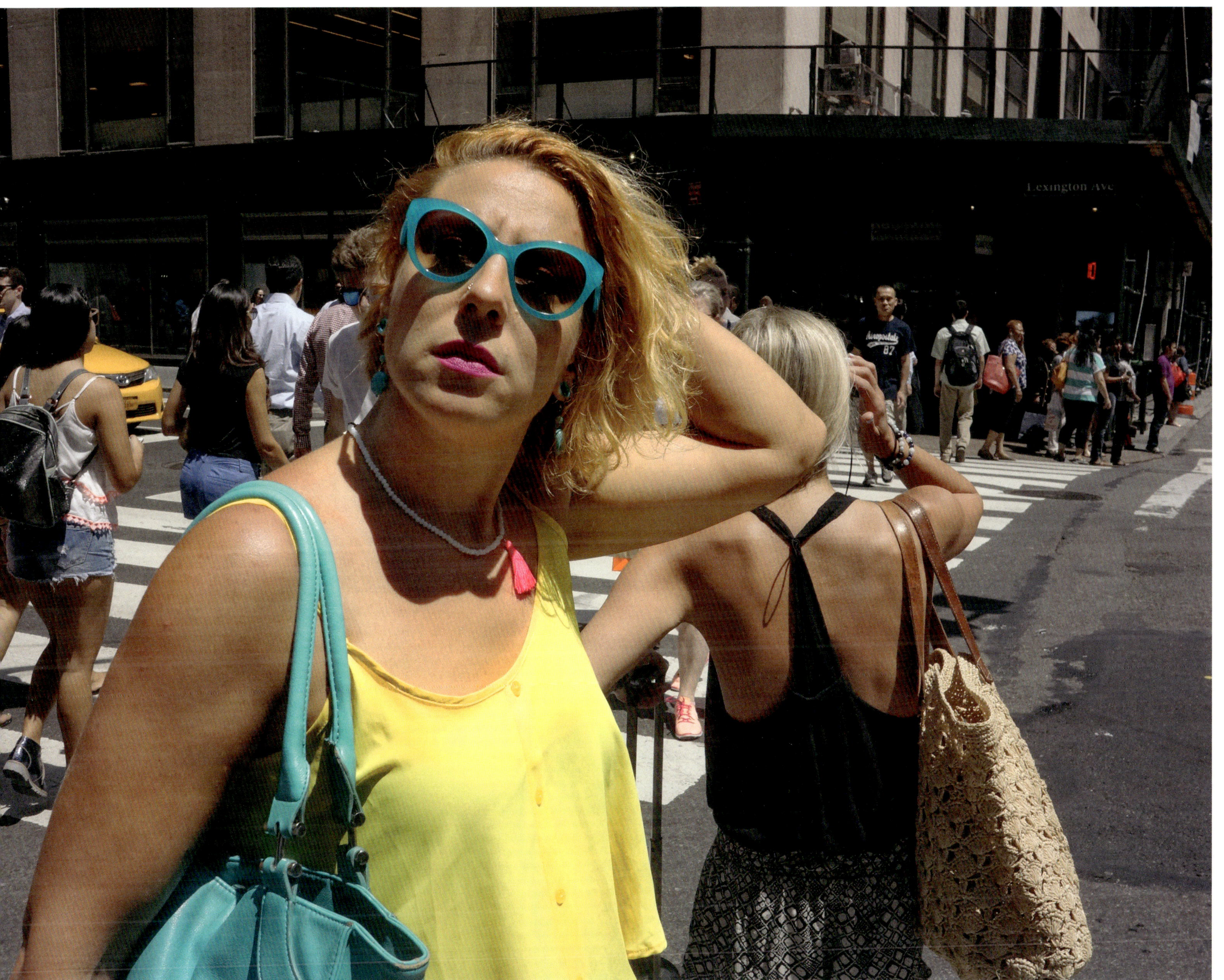

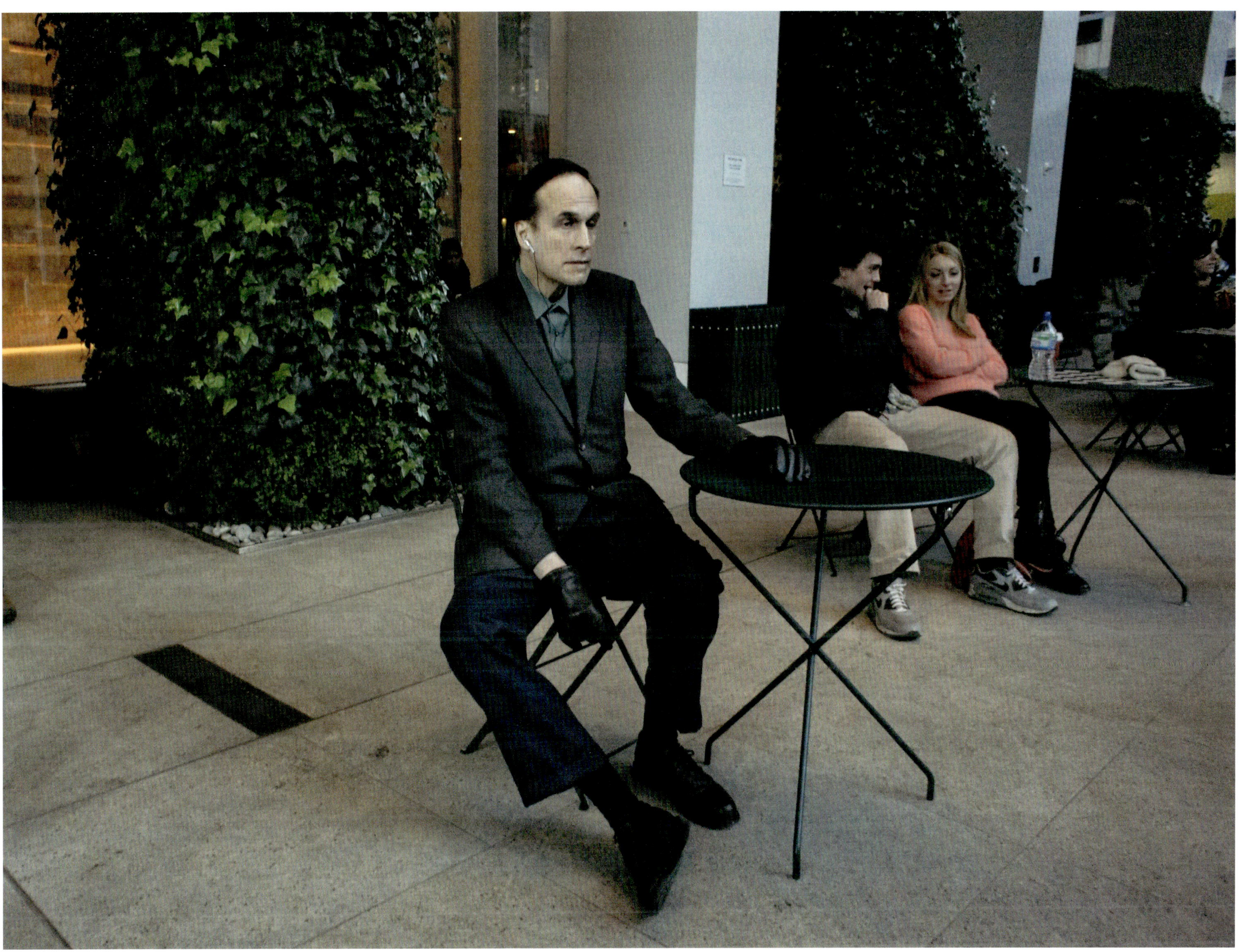

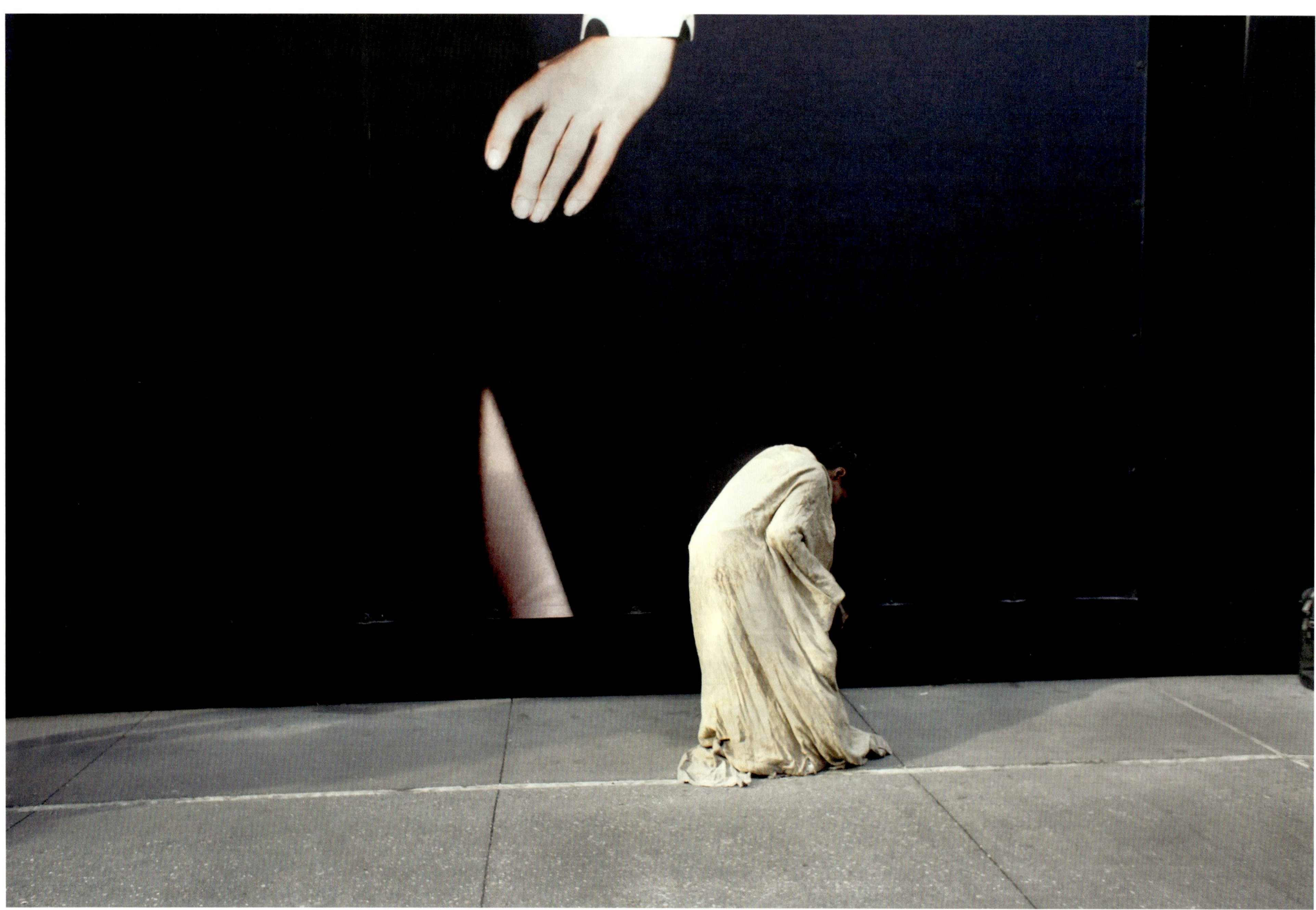

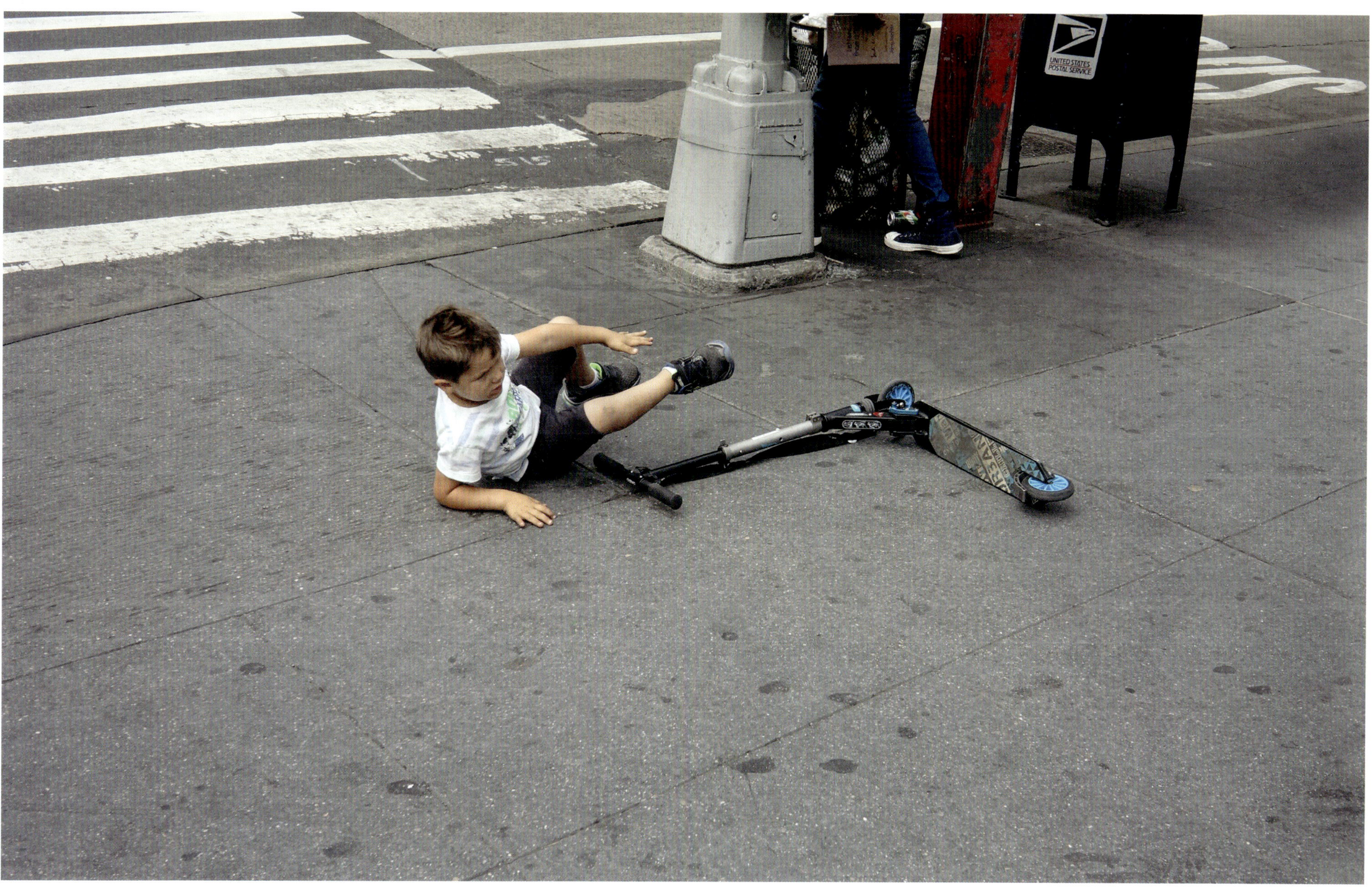

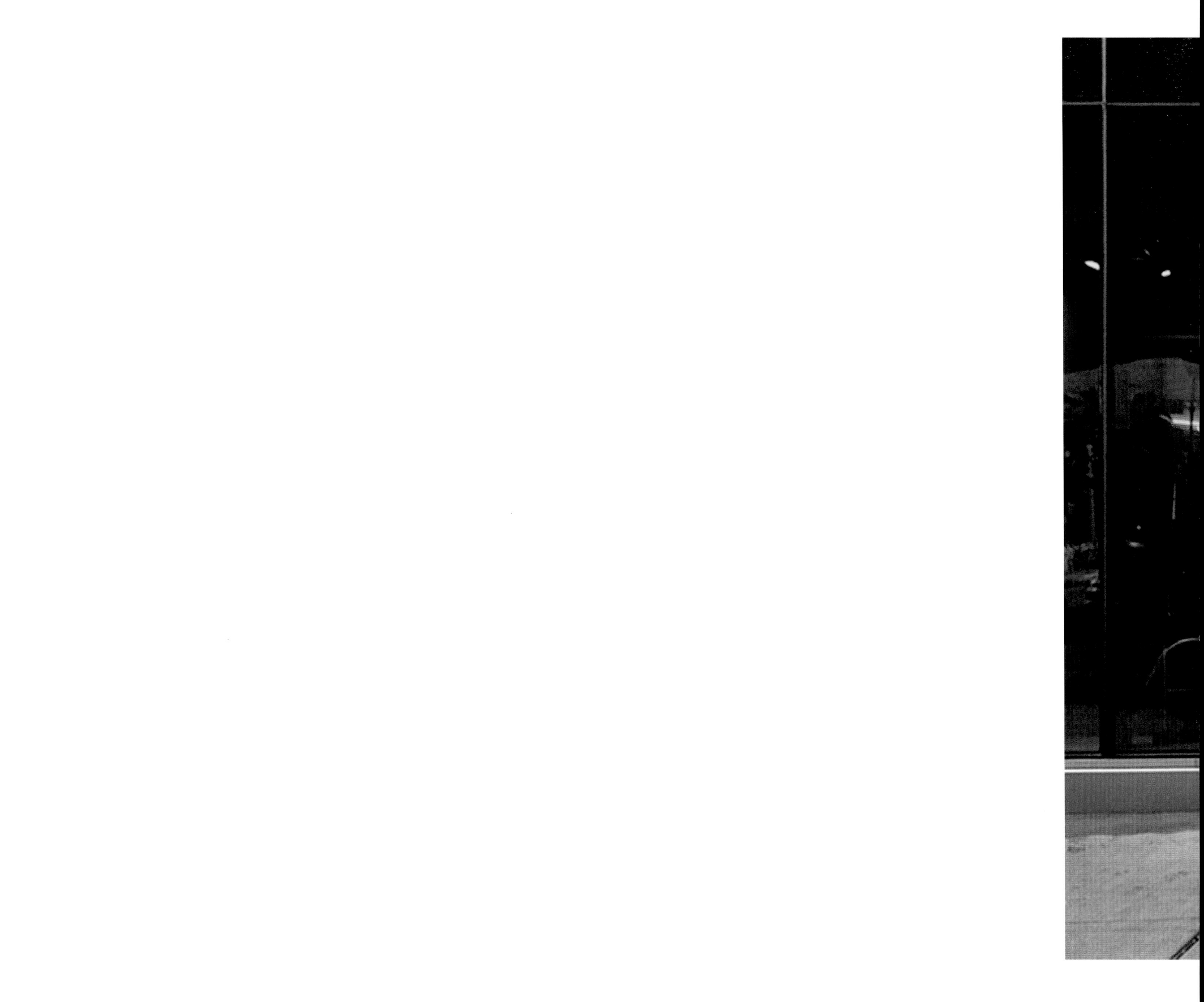

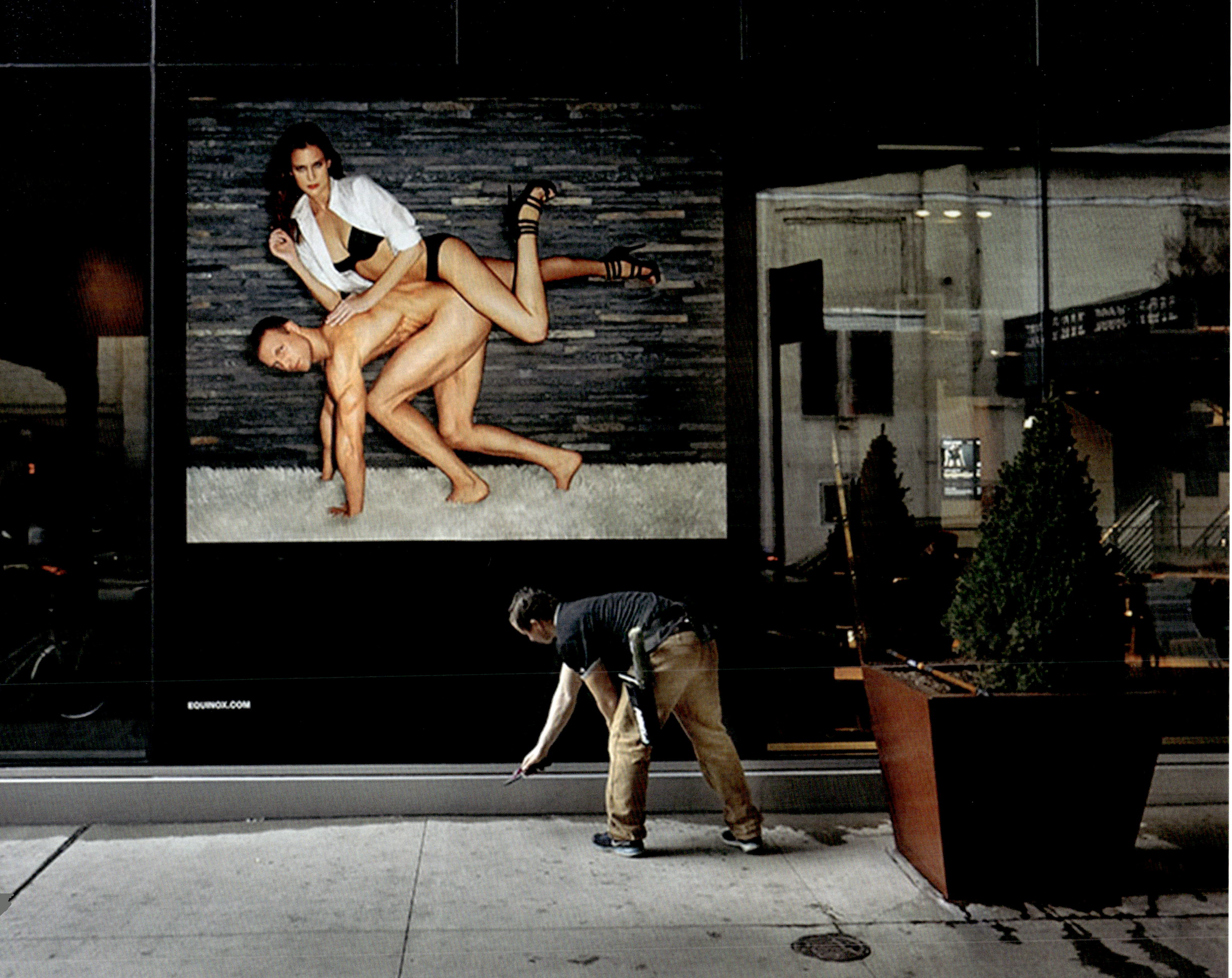

EQUINOX.COM

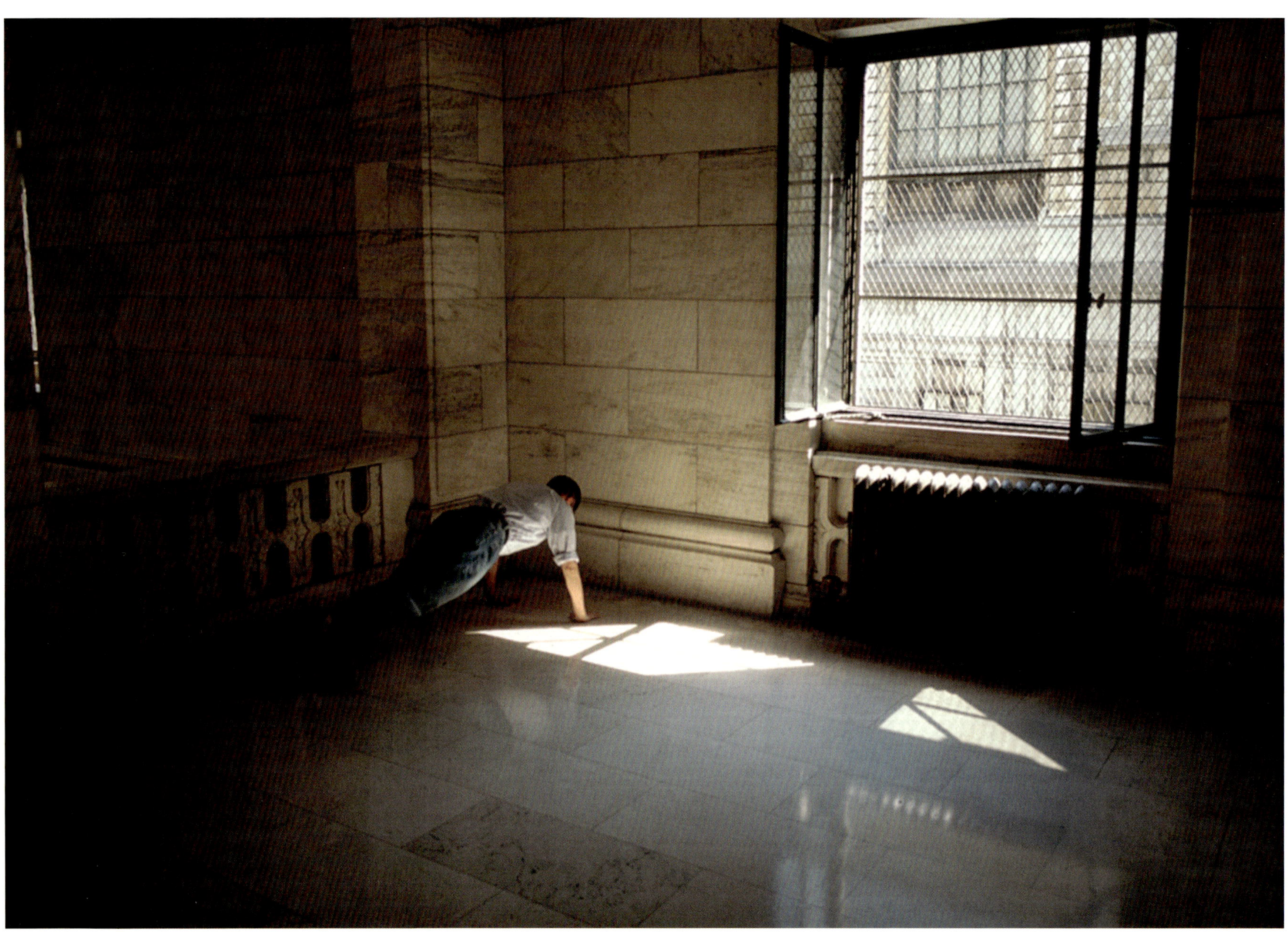

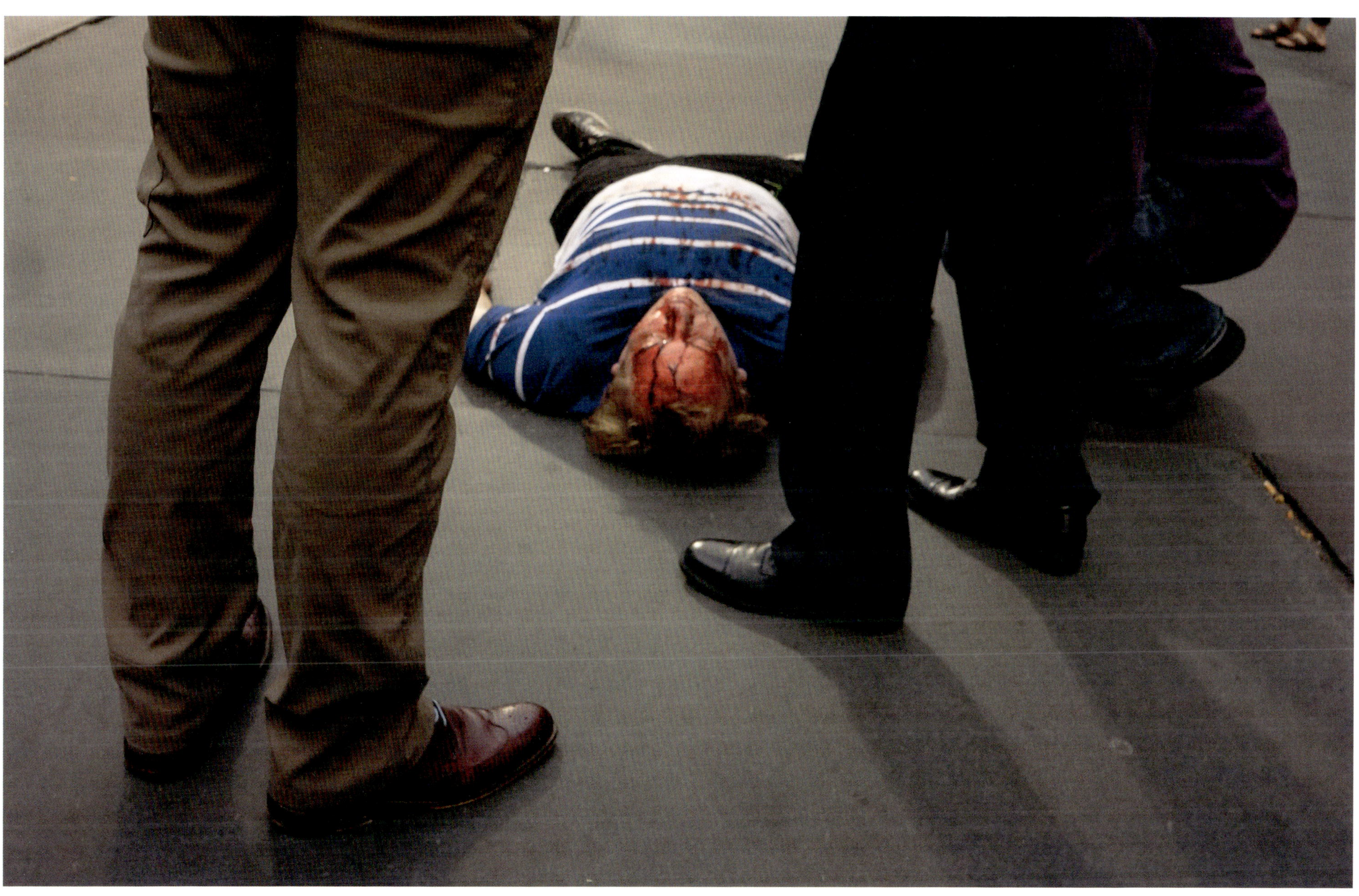

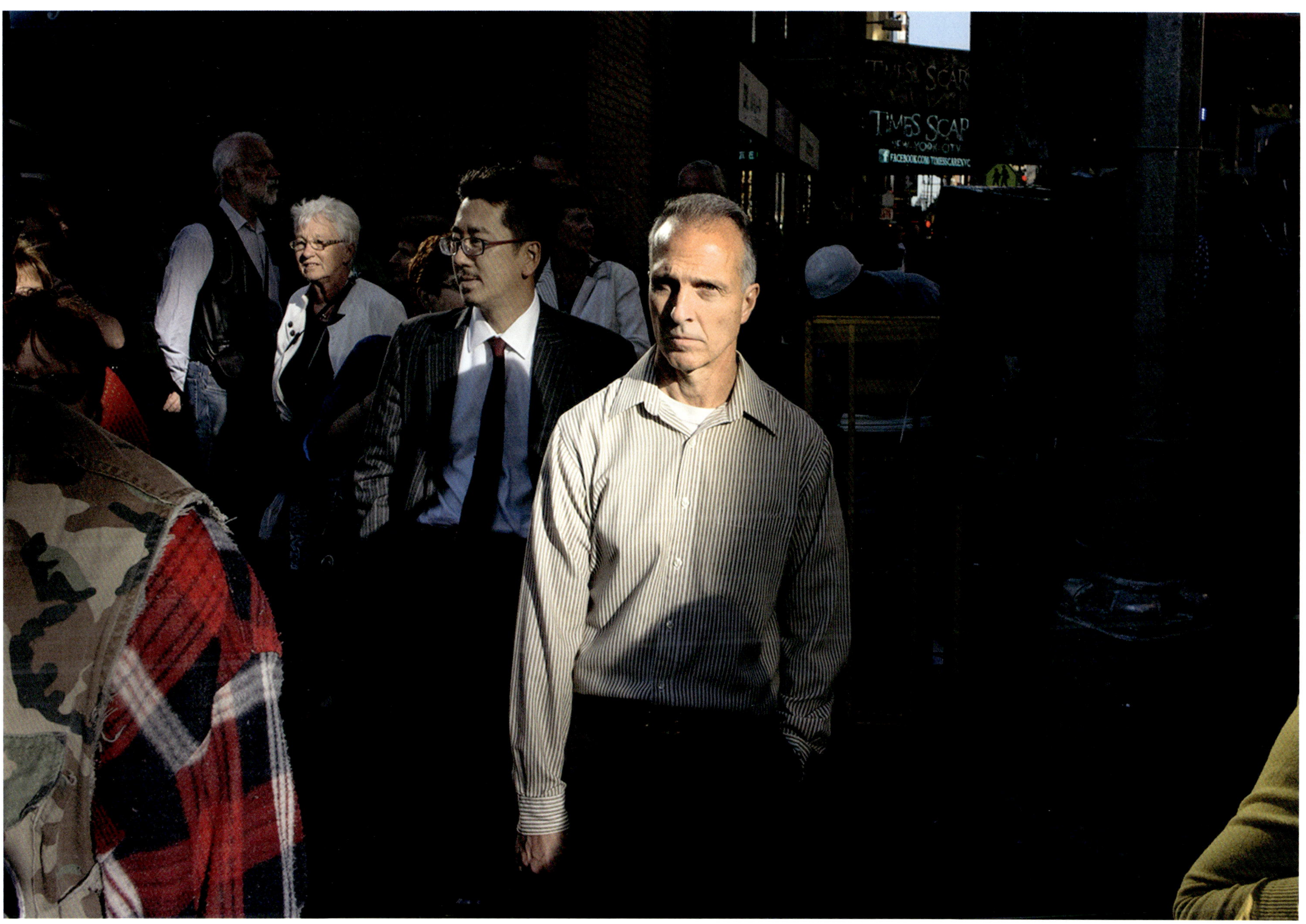
TIMES SCAR
TIMES SCAR
NEW YORK CITY
FACEBOOK.COM/TIMESCARENYC

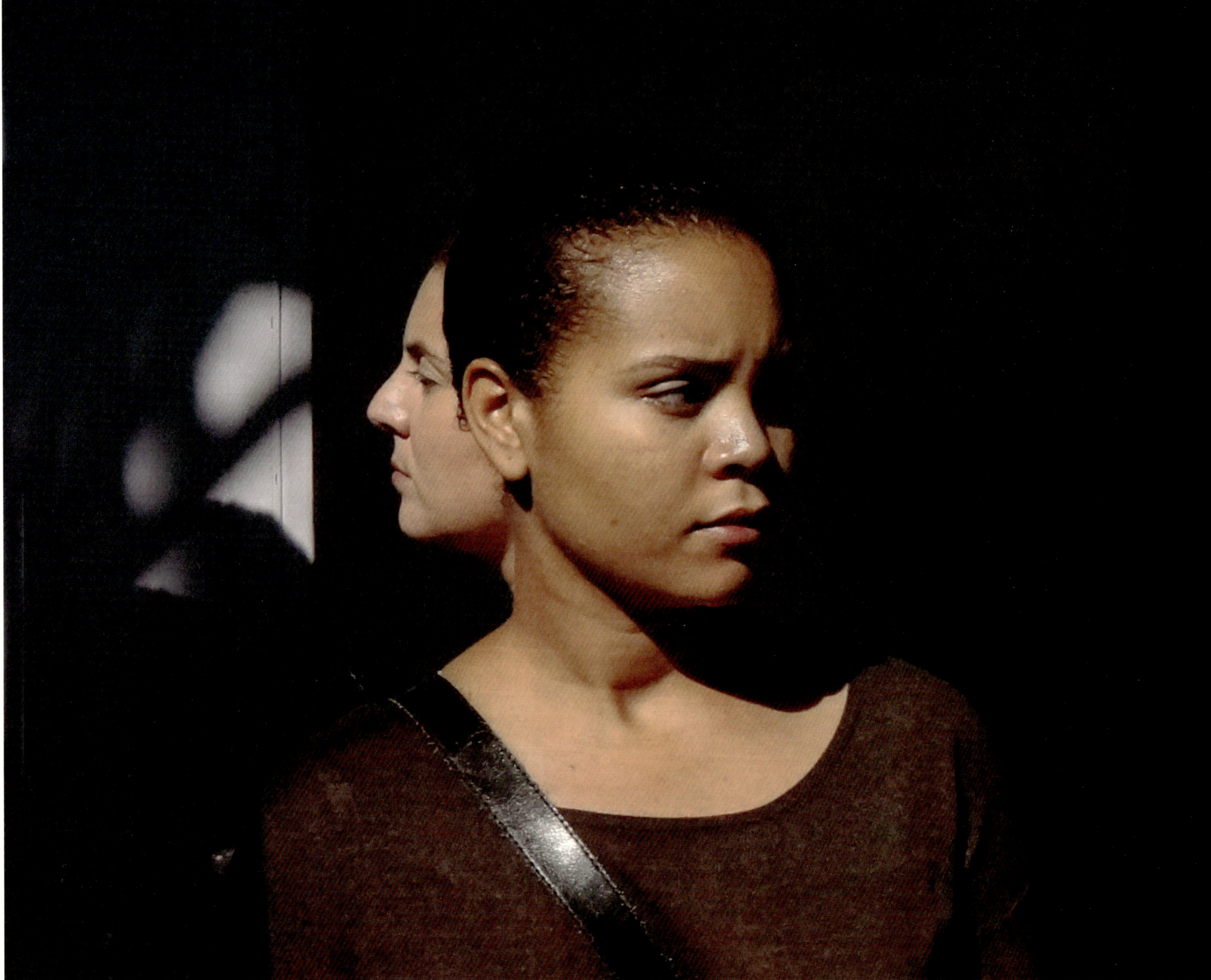

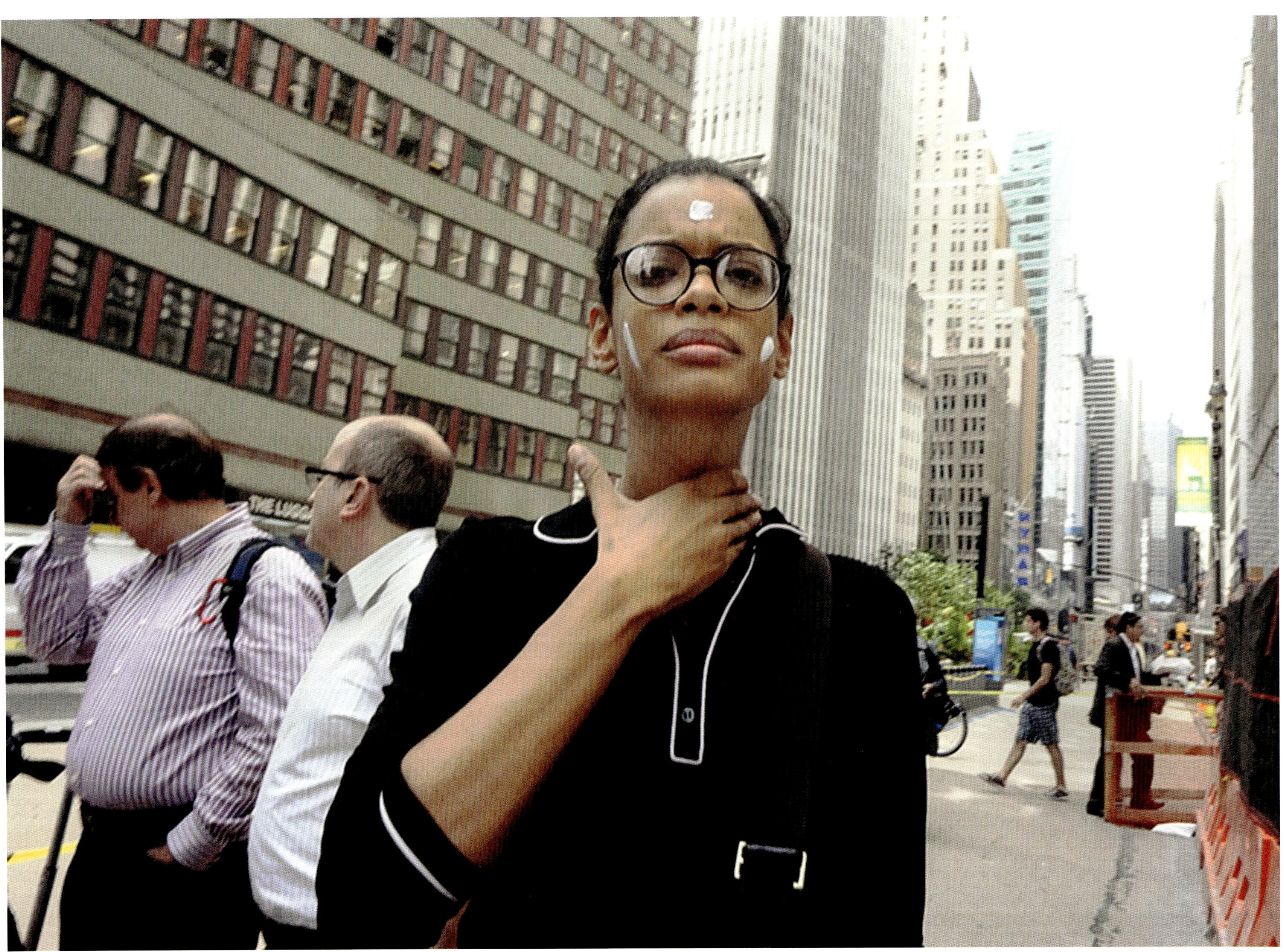

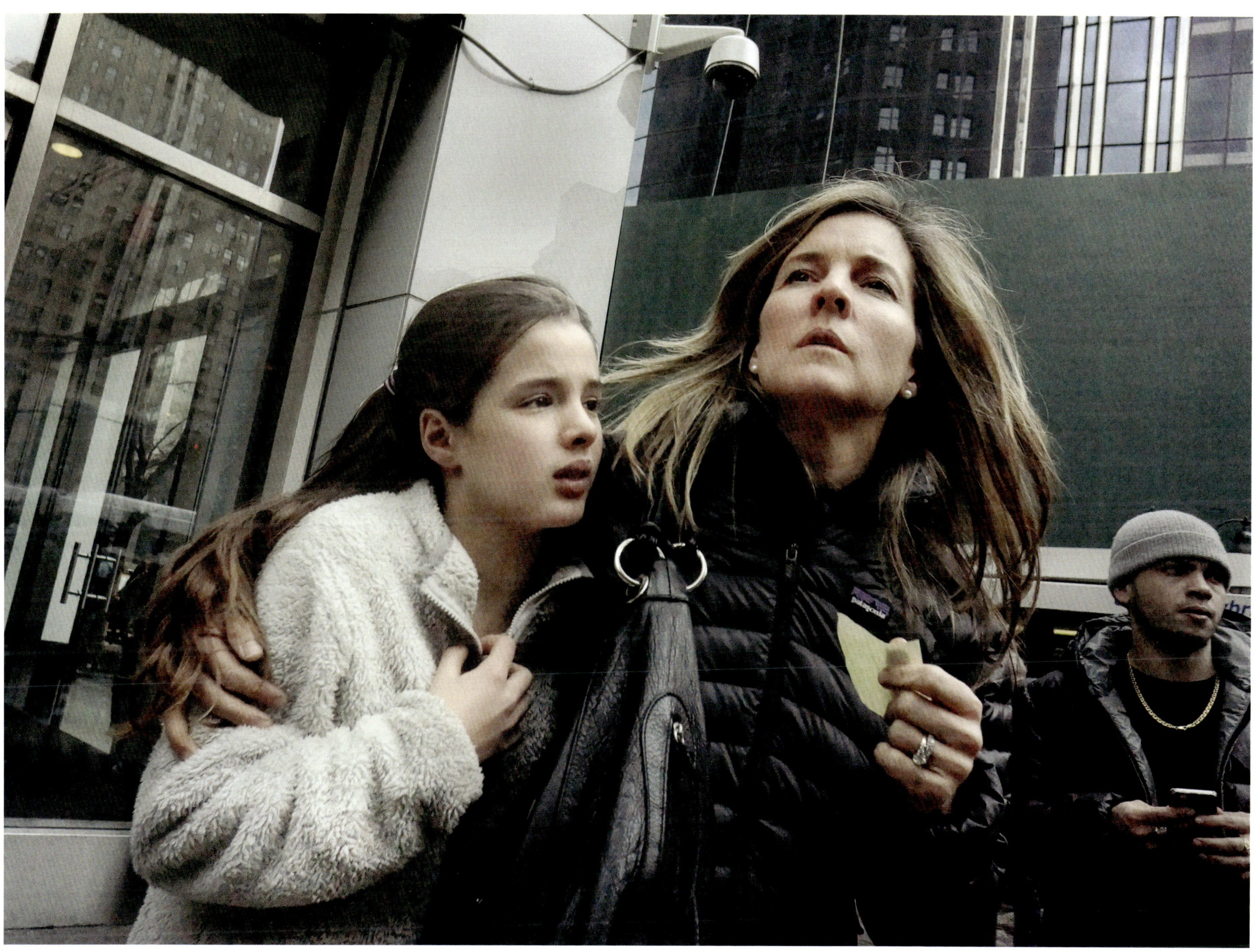

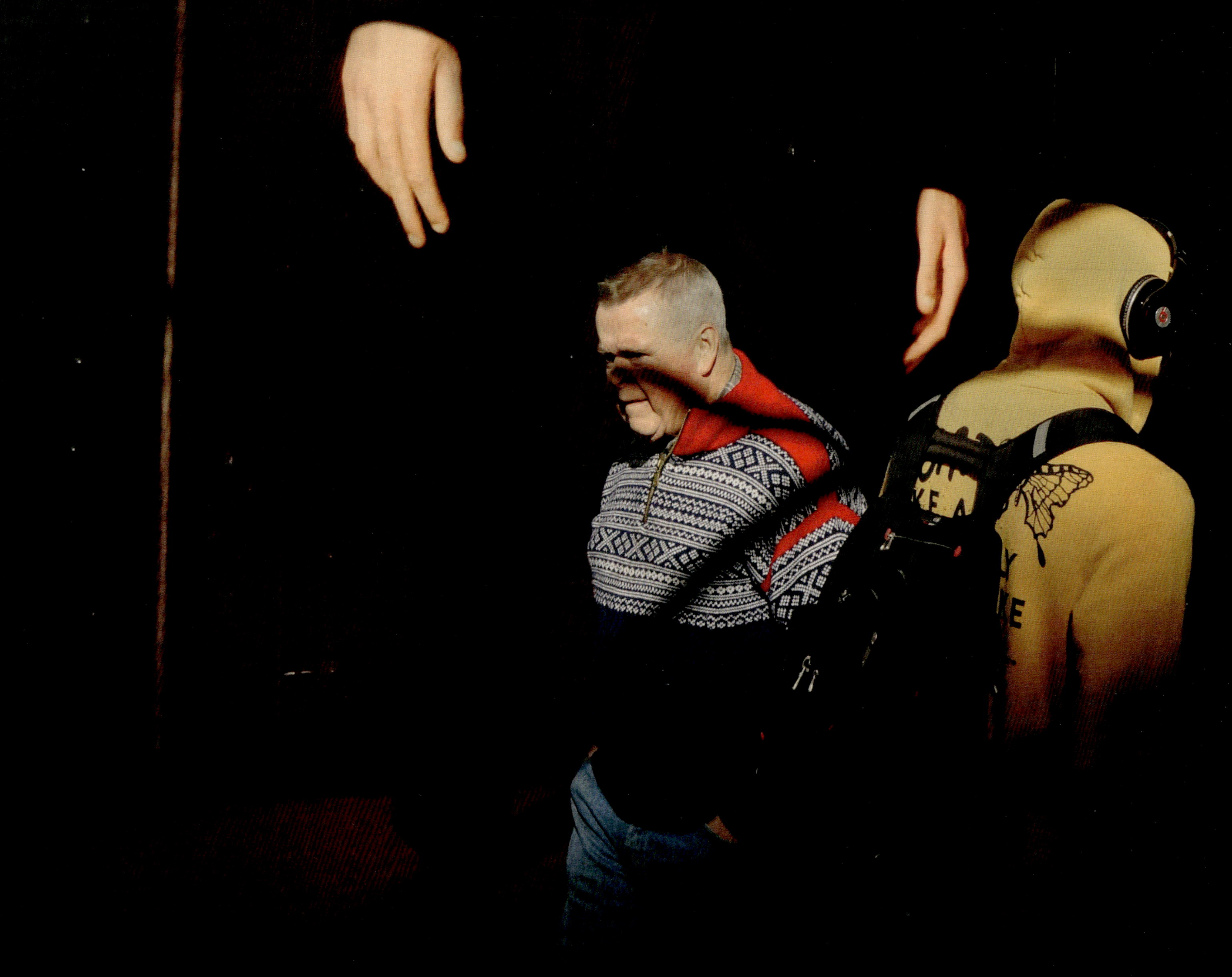

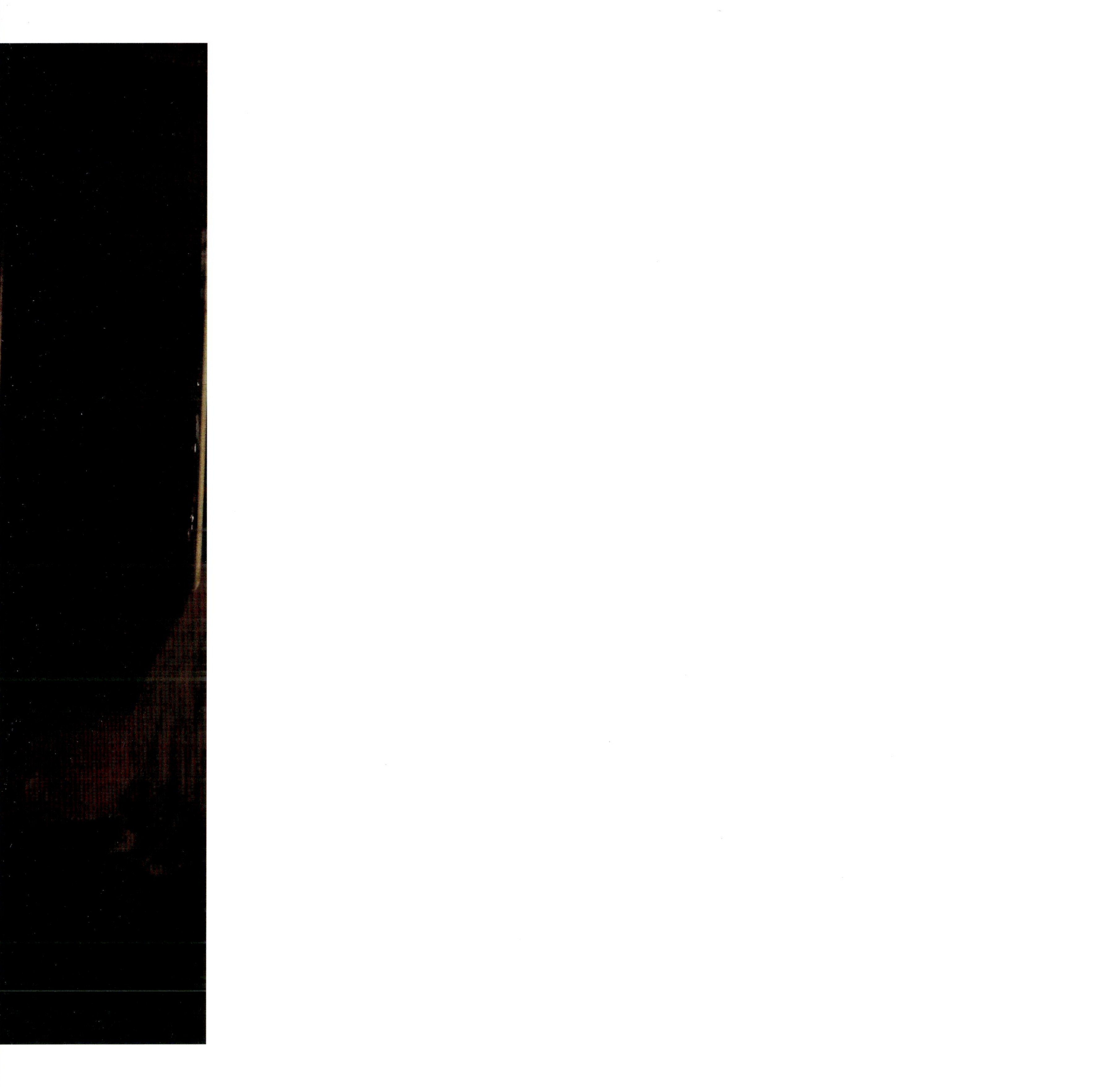

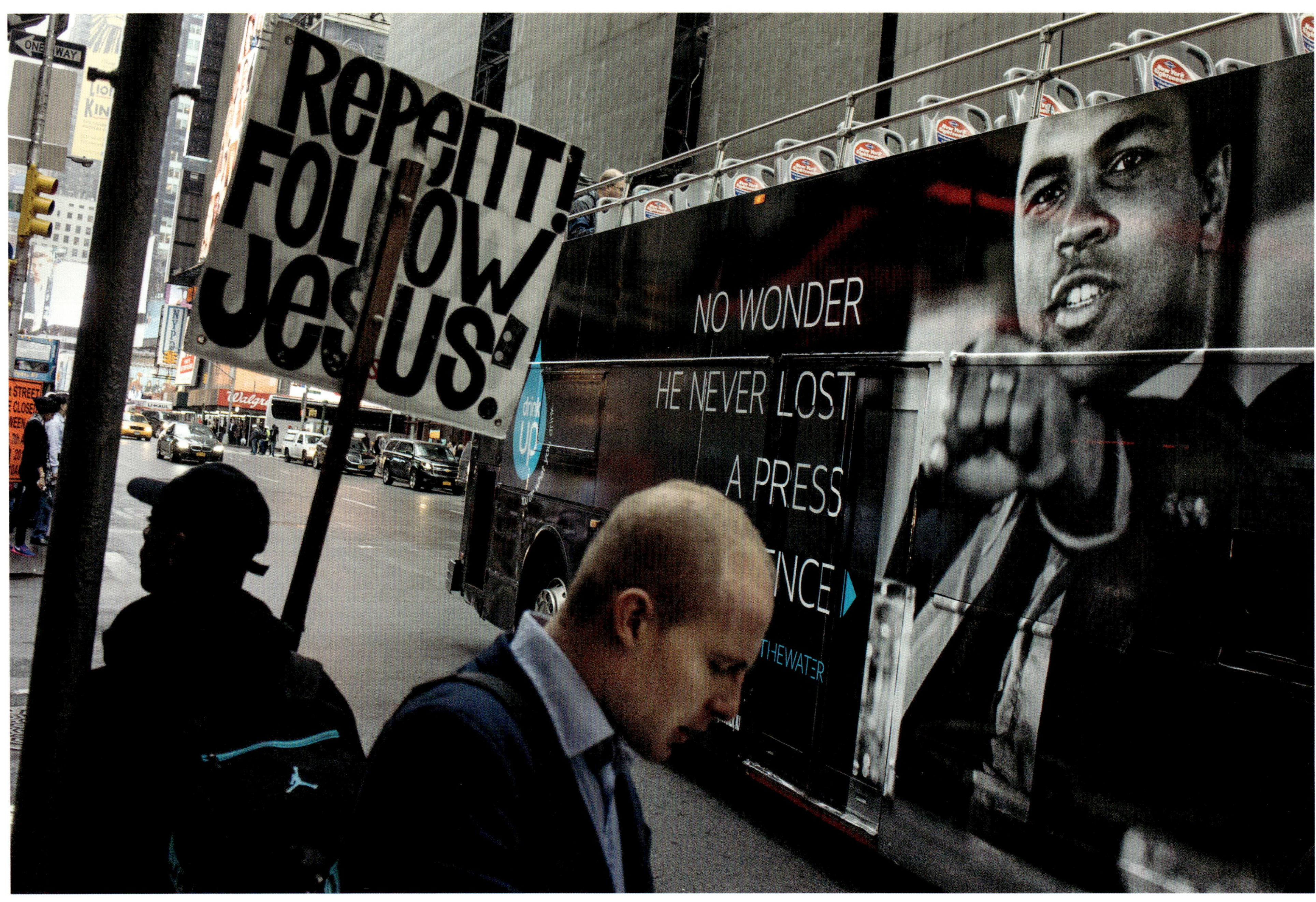
Repent!
FOLLOW
JeSUS!
NO WONDER
HE NEVER LOST
A PRESS
ENCE
THEWATER
ONE WAY
LION
KING

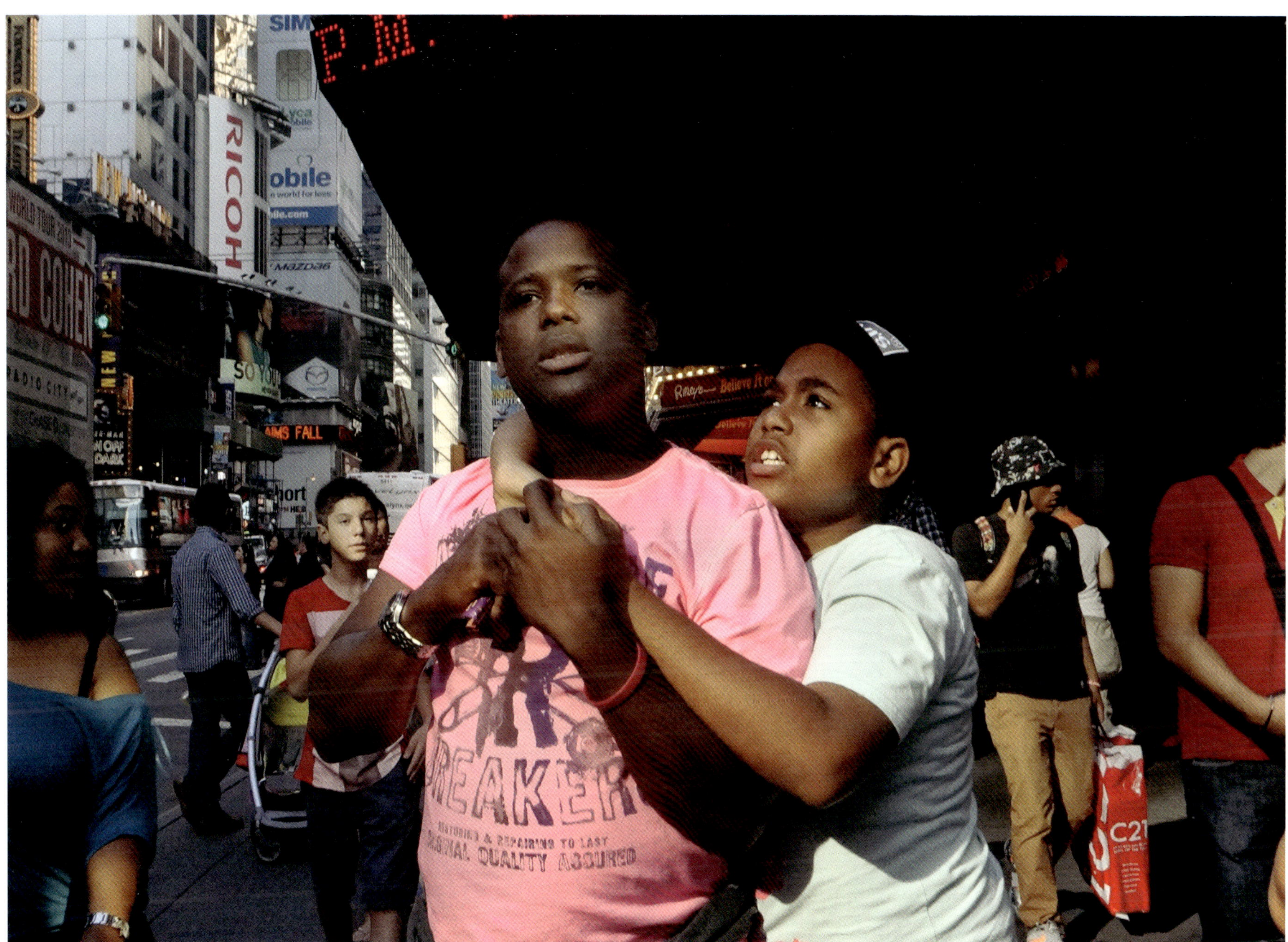

P.M.
SIM
RICOH
obile
a world for less
bile.com
WORLD TOUR 2010
RD COHEN
RADIO CITY
SO YOU
AIMS FALL
Ripley's Believe It or
C21

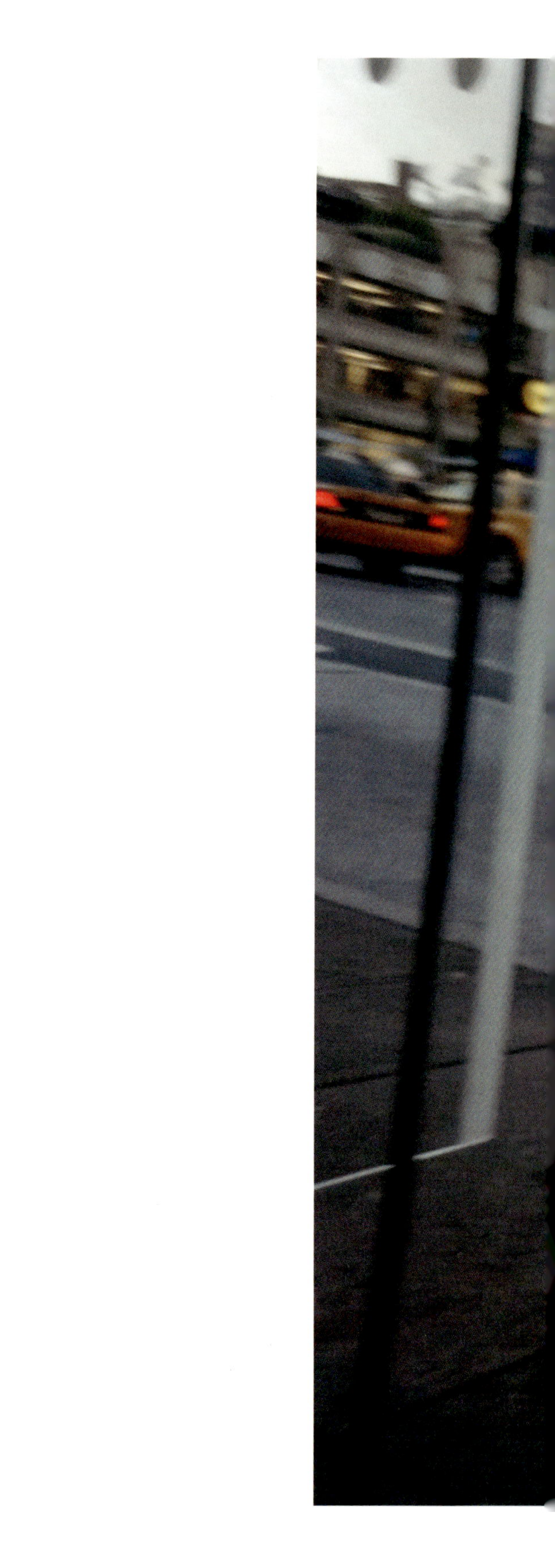

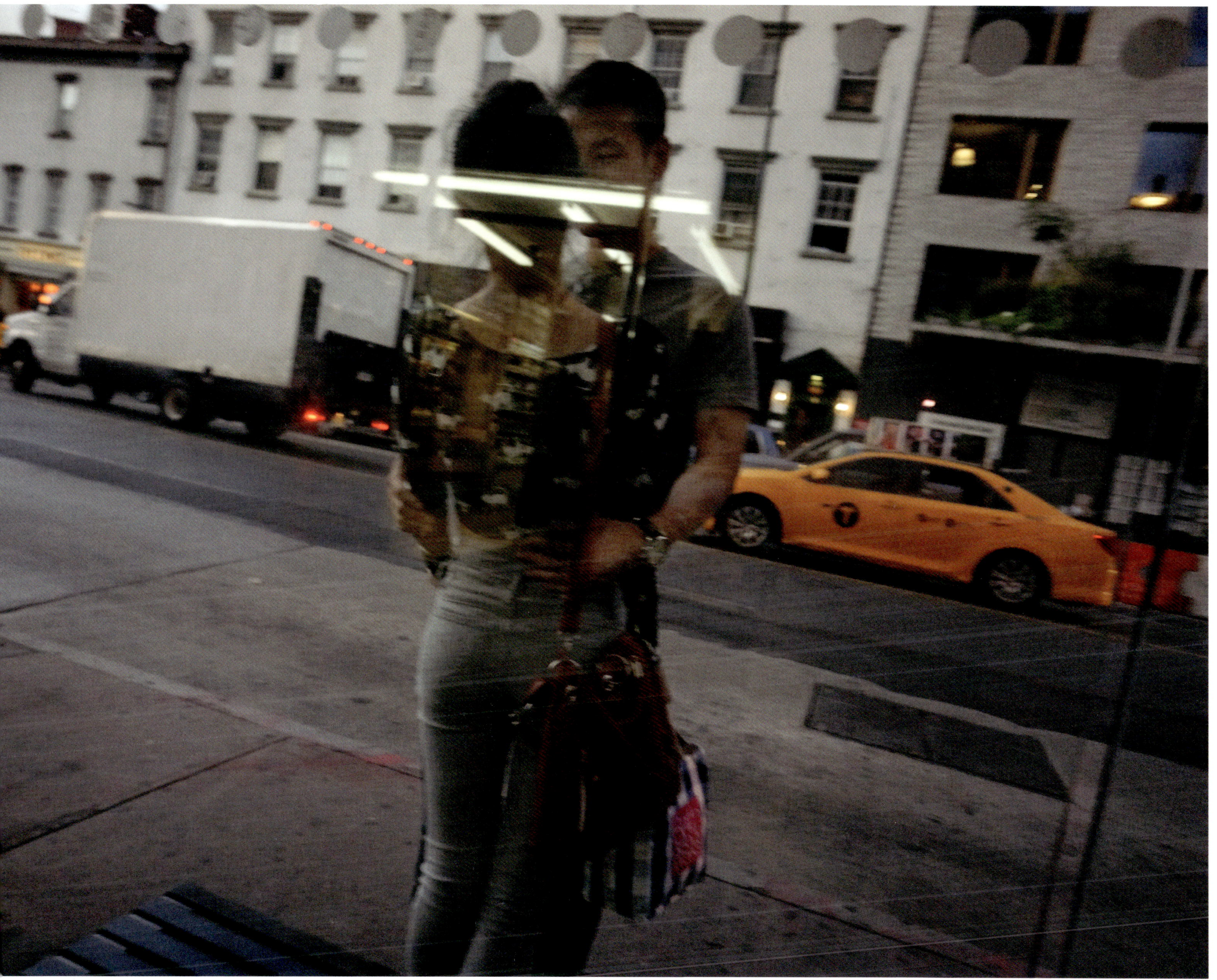

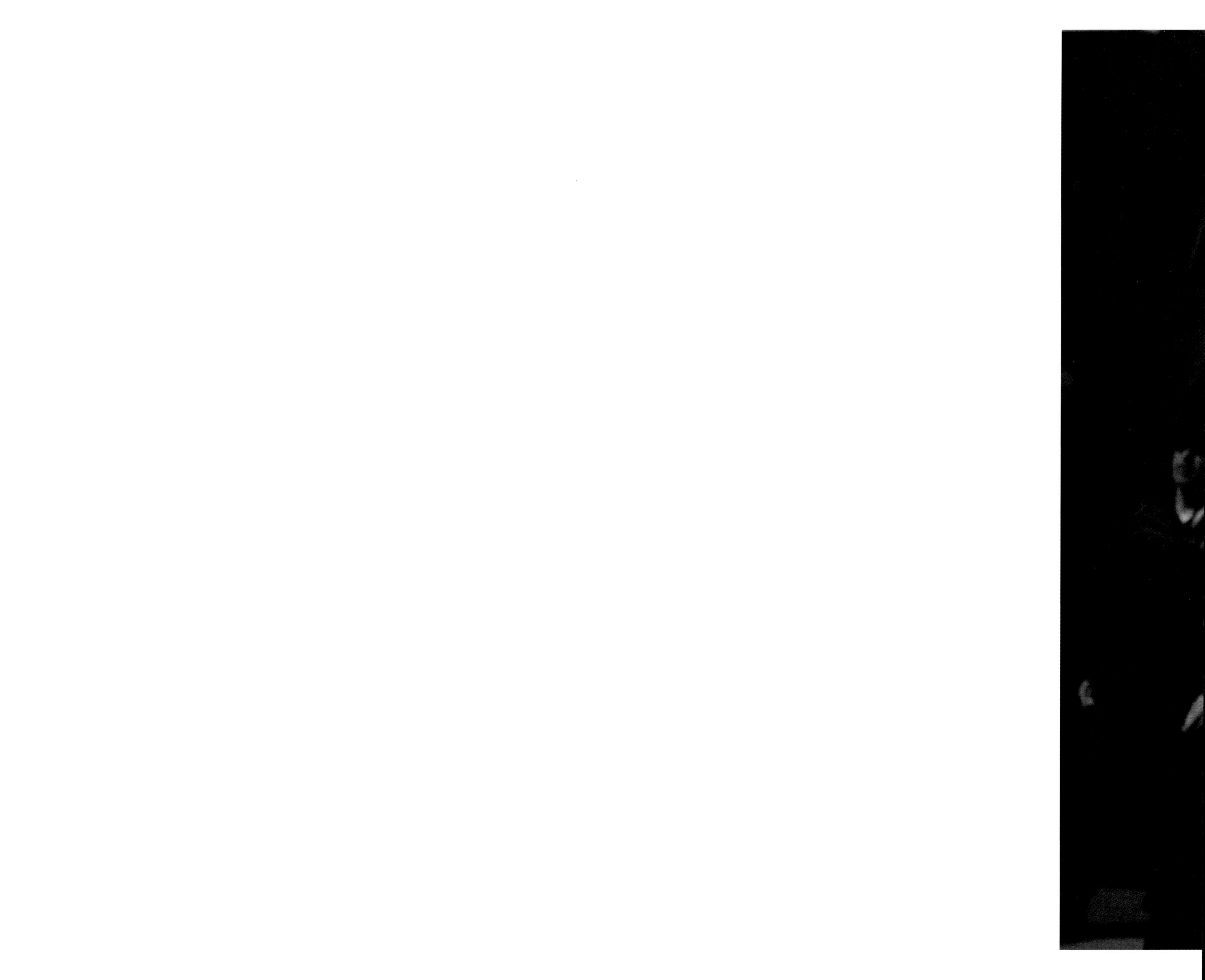

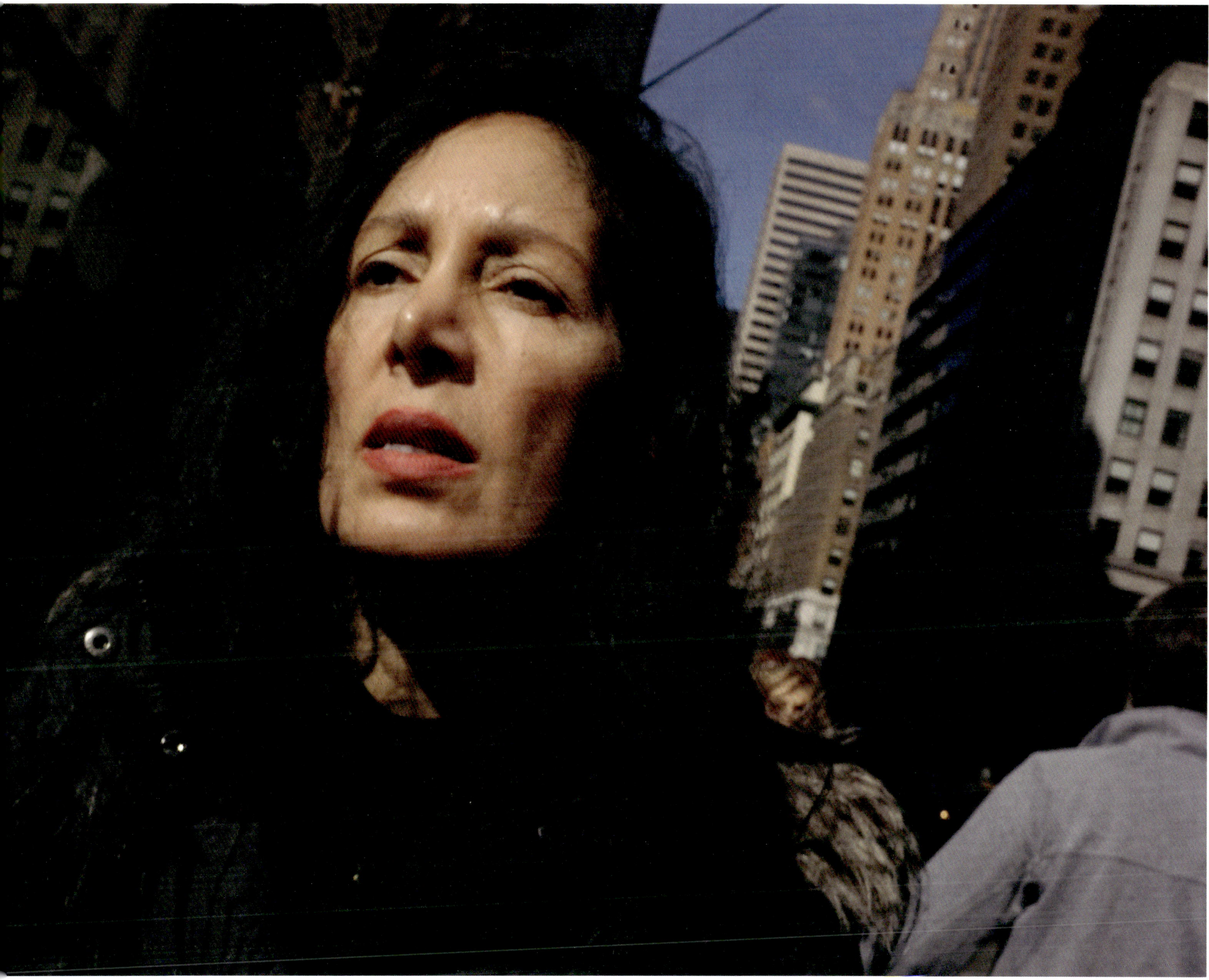

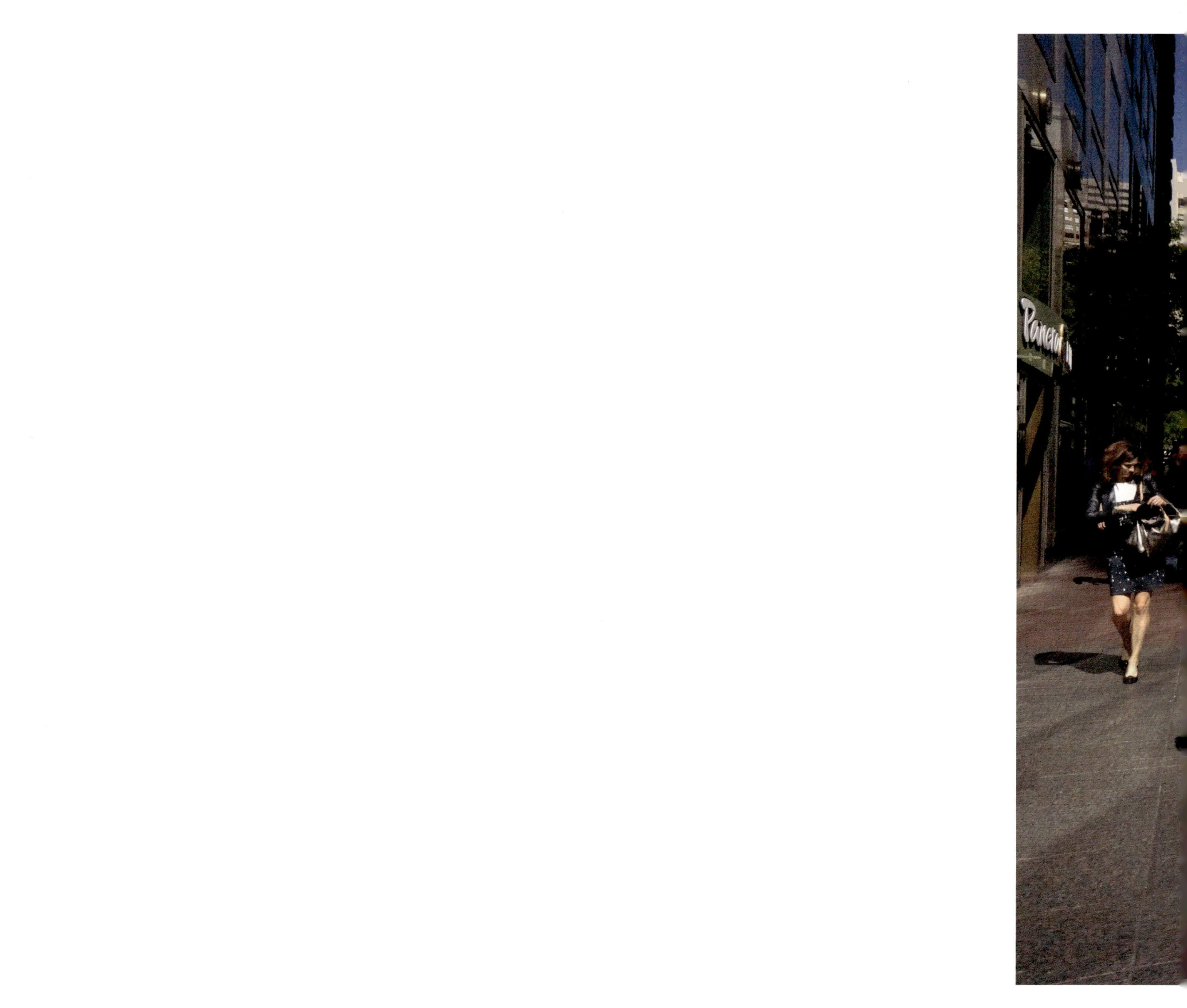

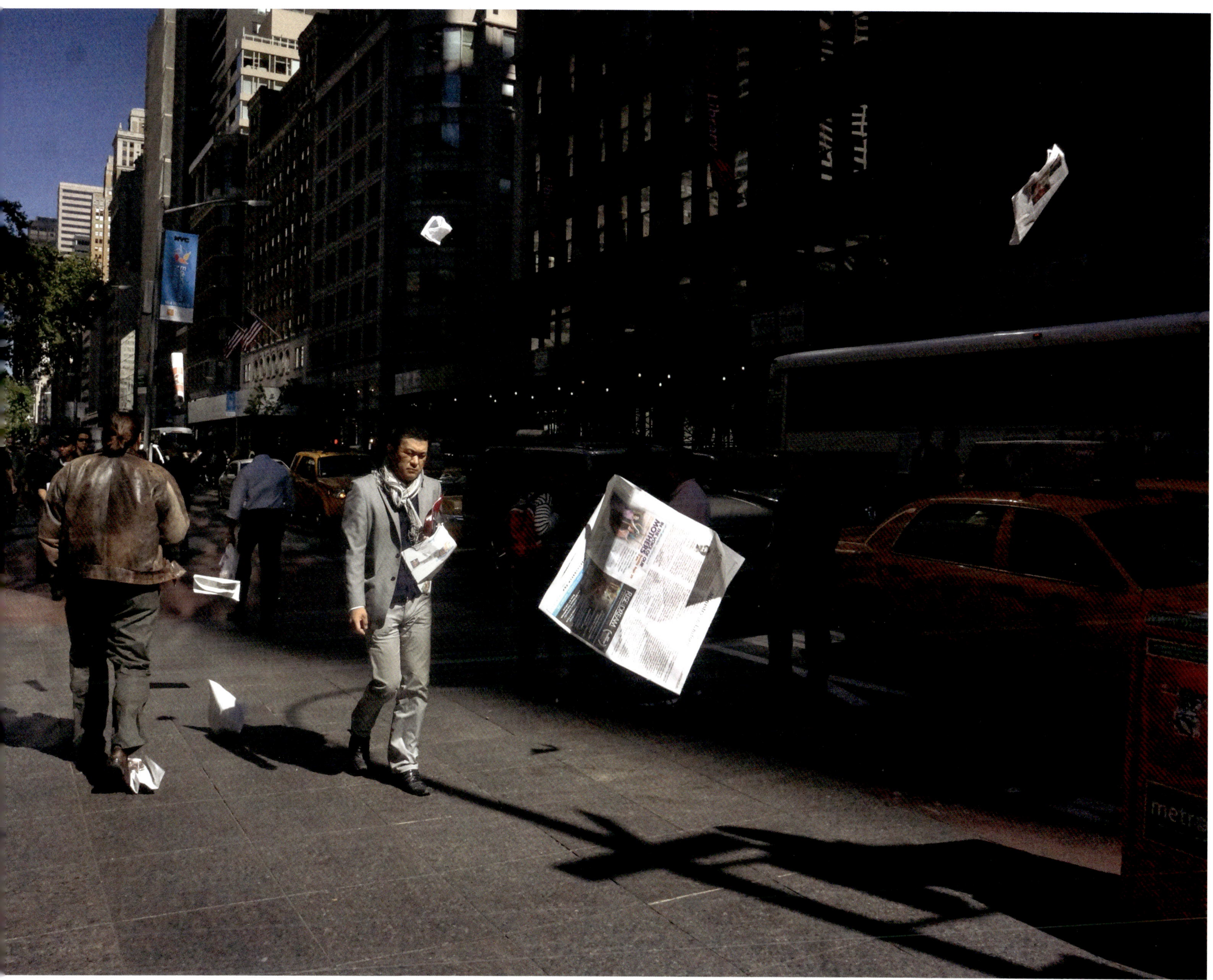

CLOUD CHAMBER

New things, different things, happen only because of what happened just a moment before. Our actions reflect and bounce off each other, sometimes literally, on the streets of New York, leading to the constant evolution of events that would not happen otherwise, or elsewhere. And as you walk amid the jackhammers, the horns and the parades, inside the sense of constant emergency that can seem to exist…you sometimes find the sense of privacy. As if you were for a moment alone. And that's often where I look as I try to take my pictures, looking inside the cloud chamber of New York City.

What I find is that, for me, New York is not so much the story of people passing in their multitudes, but rather the story told as if people, in their multitudes, were speaking to me as they pass, but in my limitations I can only make out a few things every now and then. And what are they saying? What are they telling me? They are telling me the story of what it is to be alive here.

—Dan Ziskie

Special thanks to Jason Eskenazi for his help and encouragement,
Mara Catalan for pitching in with her editing,
Bonnie Briant for her ideas, her hard work and patience
and to Andrea Albertini for making it possible.

Dan Ziskie
Cloud Chamber

Book Design by
Bonnie Briant, NYC

Published by
Damiani
info@damianieditore.com
www.damianieditore.com

Printed in April 2017 by Grafiche Damiani – Faenza Group SpA, Italy.

ISBN 978-88-6208-547-2